CREATIVE MUSIC for the CLASSROOM TEACHER

CREATIVE MUSIC *for the* CLASSROOM TEACHER

JAMES T. LUCK *Tarrant County Junior College District*

RANDOM HOUSE New York

We gratefully acknowledge the following publishers and agents for permission to reprint these songs:

"Hoo! Hoo!" from *New Songs and Games* by Ethel Crowninshield. Reprinted by permission of the Boston Music Company.

"How Do You Do?" from *Music for Young Americans*, book 2, by Richard C. Berg, Daniel S. Hooley, Robert W. Pace, and Josephine Wolverton. Reprinted by permission of the American Book Publishing Company.

"My Home's in Montana" from *Singing Cowboy* by Margaret Larkin, published by Oak Publications. Copyright 1931 by Alfred A. Knopf, Inc. Reprinted by permission of Barthold Fles, Literary Agent.

"Walk Along John" from *The American Play-Party Song Book* originally published in the University Studies of the University of Nebraska, now published by Frederick Unger Publishing Co., Inc. Copyright 1937, © 1965 by B. A. Botkin. New material Copyright © 1963 by B. A. Botkin. Reprinted by permission of Curtis Brown, Ltd.

Published in the United States by Random House, Inc., New York, and simultaneously in Canada by Random House of Canada Limited, Toronto.

ISBN: 0–394–30369–5
Library of Congress Catalog Card Number: 73–127646

Manufactured in the United States of America. Printed and bound by The Kingsport Press, Kingsport, Tenn.

First Edition
987654321

Preface

This book has been written primarily to provide experiences with music creativity for the college student majoring in elementary education and for the "in-service" classroom teacher. It is felt that the student majoring in music education will find this as excellent supplementary material. As in any area where skills are concerned, the greater the basic theoretical knowledge a person has, the more satisfying his experiences with the creative process are likely to be. However, it is felt that because of the unique approach to music creativity found in this book, which requires only the most elemental knowledge of music fundamentals, students with limited backgrounds in music can realize highly successful musical experiences. The apparent dearth of vital and exciting musical activities in the elementary classroom can be traced in part to the fact that many teachers feel insecure and lack confidence when it comes to leading children in this kind of classroom performance. It is felt that this condition can be partially alleviated if a teacher has had experiences in creating music in the form of rhythmic activities, singing and playing melodies, and harmonic accompaniments.

In this book creativity is an evolutionary process—the student works from an existing melody taken from children's literature and, in a step-by-step procedure, creates rhythmic patterns, melodic descants, and harmonic accompaniments. By being involved in writing music which can subsequently be used in her own classroom situations, the teacher should gain much needed confidence and skill. The creative procedures described herein will give the teacher opportunities to acquire knowledge and examine material necessary to carry on a more extensive study of music within the classroom.

Throughout this book the term ORCHESTRATION (which traditionally means "the arrangement of music for instruments of the symphony orchestra") is used to mean the arrangement of music literature for use with children in the elementary school classroom where activities in rhythm, melody, and harmony are sought and planned. These arrangements may vary from simple presentations of rhythmic activities extracted from simple tunes to complete orchestrations of activities involving one-, two-, or three-part singing, playing of rhythm and melody instruments simultaneously, and harmonic accompaniments for various fretted instruments, autoharp, and piano.

This book contains four parts: Rhythm, Melody, Harmonic Accompaniment, and Completed Orchestrations. Each of the first three parts is divided into (I) Theory and Analysis, (II) Application, and (III) Assignments: Student Worksheets. The Theory and Analysis sections are concerned with the definition of terms and procedures. The Application sections include examples of the area previously discussed. The Assignments sections allow students to begin the creative process in each of the musical elements around which the book is structured. The examples and orchestrations provide immediate source materials to be used in completing the assigned worksheets. They also provide music material which may be used in future classroom situations. The following example serves to suggest ways in which a completed orchestration might be used in an actual elementary school classroom:

> On one day of a particular week the musical activity might be devoted entirely to rhythm. The teacher could use a completed orchestration as the basis for her musical activity. Rhythmic evolvements could be extracted and dealt with as the principal activity of the period. This could be repeated on other days of the week, shifting to other orchestrated tunes. To make the lesson more interesting, and to fulfill one of the basic tenets of elementary music education, other days of the week could be devoted to singing the existing melodies and gradually progressing to the point of adding the newly created descants. Thus, part-singing activities could be initiated. Since these same melodies also provide material for the use of melody instruments, melody instruments could be utilized in a separate activity or could be used in conjunction with vocal performances. The performance of the entire orchestration, then, could be projected as a goal for the students and as a focal point for all their endeavors. As a result of learning to follow their parts on these orchestrations, the children will develop skill in reading music.

Acknowledgments

To my loyal and dedicated students, who have conscientiously supported the philosophy found in this work by giving unstintingly of their time to work out a myriad of details in the class development of this project, and to my faithful and zealous secretary, Patsy Nicholson, for the invaluable assistance given me in manuscript preparation, I wish to express my profound gratitude. To my colleagues of the Fine Arts Staff of Tarrant County Junior College District, and especially Dr. J. T. Matthews, for their advice, criticism, and encouragement, I also want to express my appreciation.

The song literature found in this workbook is included in most music books for children. Their firm position in standard repertoire can be attributed to the many teachers who have sung and taught them to our children down through the years.

Contents

Part 1

RHYTHM

1 Theory and Analysis

The aim of this part is to teach the procedures for evolving rhythmic patterns from existing melodies and for scoring these patterns for rhythmic activities. These activities, when used in the elementary classroom, will help children to hear and feel the beat of music, will develop in them rhythmic sensitivity and coordination, and will give them the experience of actually playing different kinds of rhythmic patterns on percussion instruments.

A. Definition of Terms

1 *Meter Rhythm (M.R.)*

Meter signatures indicate the number of basic pulsations to each measure of music. METER RHYTHM is the notation of these pulsations in musical symbols. Hereafter, meter rhythm is referred to as M.R.

There are two classifications of meter signatures: simple and compound. Below are examples of frequently used meters showing how they are notated to indicate M.R.:

SIMPLE METERS

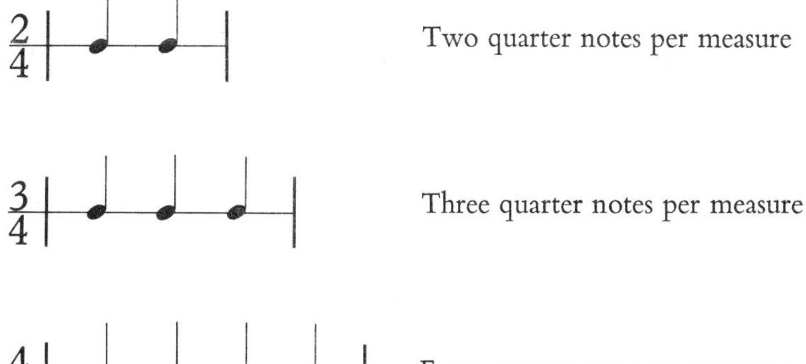

Two quarter notes per measure

Three quarter notes per measure

Four quarter notes per measure

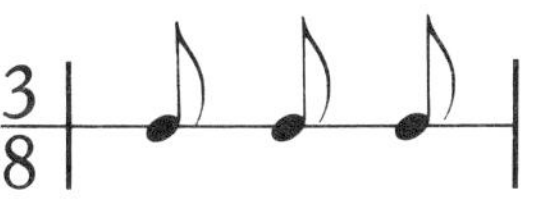

Three eighth notes per measure

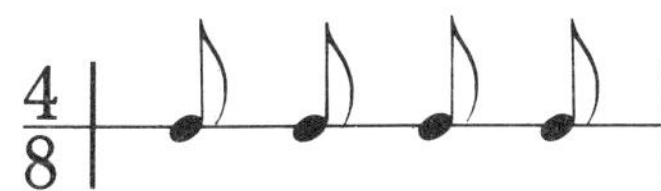

Four eighth notes per measure

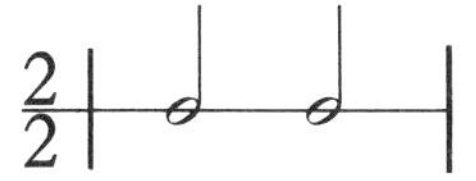

Two half notes per measure

COMPOUND METERS

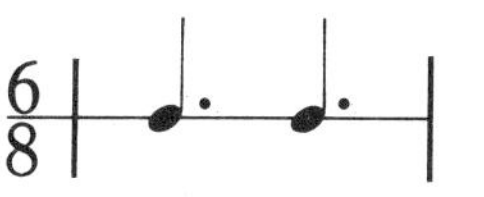

Two dotted quarter notes per measure

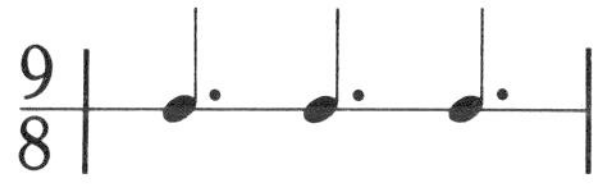

Three dotted quarter notes per measure

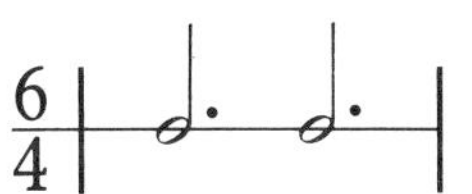

Two dotted half notes per measure

It should be noted that the meters *most* frequently used in music literature for children are:

$$\frac{2}{4}, \frac{3}{4}, \frac{4}{4}, \frac{6}{8}$$

2 *Characteristic Rhythm (C.R.)*

CHARACTERISTIC RHYTHMS are those rhythmic patterns which are typical and distinctive in a melodic line. The most obvious patterns are those which stand out so conspicuously in a song that they are actually "heard" or "felt" as the melody is performed. Every melody is structured with these "characteristic" rhythmic patterns. Some patterns fall easily into one-measure limitations, others constitute only a portion of a measure. Many melodies have patterns which are definitely longer than one measure duration.

The following examples illustrate how various characteristic rhythms can be extracted from melodies which can subsequently be used in creating rhythmic activities:

Example 1: THE BLUE-TAIL FLY

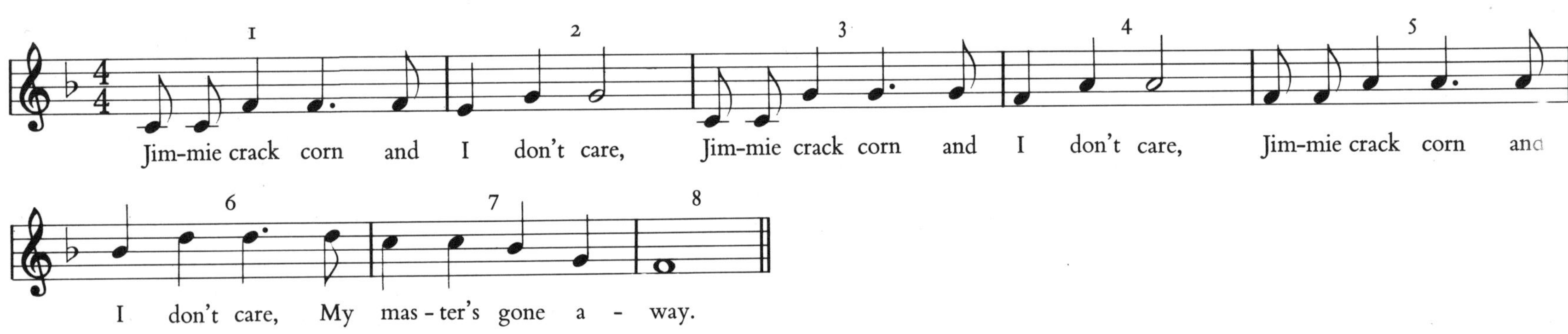
1
2
3
4
5
Jim-mie crack corn and I don't care, Jim-mie crack corn and I don't care, Jim-mie crack corn and
6
7
8
I don't care, My mas - ter's gone a - way.

The pattern found in measures 1, 3, and 5 could, because of its frequency of usage and because of its relation to the text "Jimmie crack corn," serve as a C.R.:

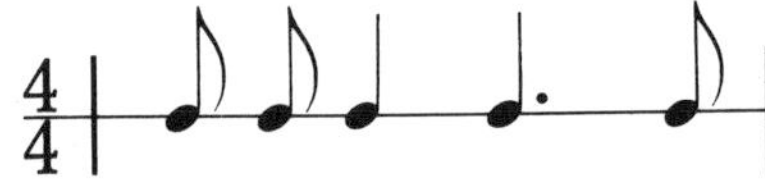

Another distinctive pattern is found in measures 2 and 4:

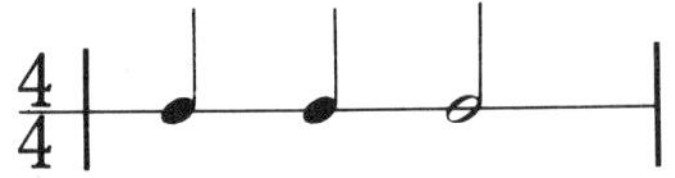

The two patterns above show patterns consuming one complete measure. If one looks further, it becomes apparent that both of these C.R.s could be grouped together to form a single rhythmic activity:

At least two additional patterns could be structured if the possibility of using fragments of measures is considered. For example, one could take the pattern of the first half of measure 1 and repeat it:

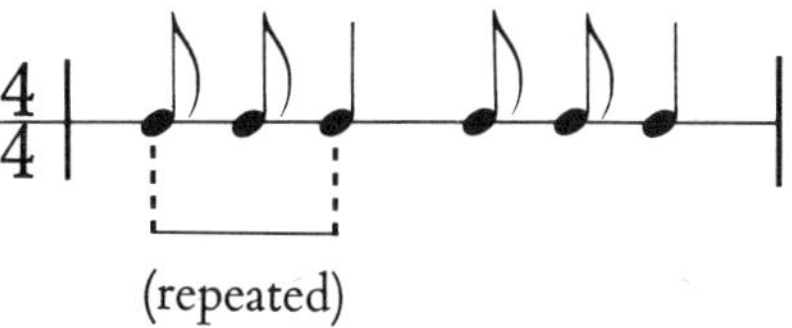
(repeated)

or the pattern of the second half of measure 1:

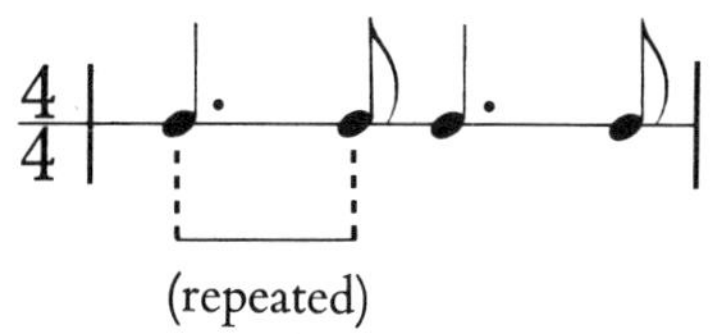
(repeated)

The following score summarizes these patterns. The "etc." indicates that they would be scored throughout the entire piece.

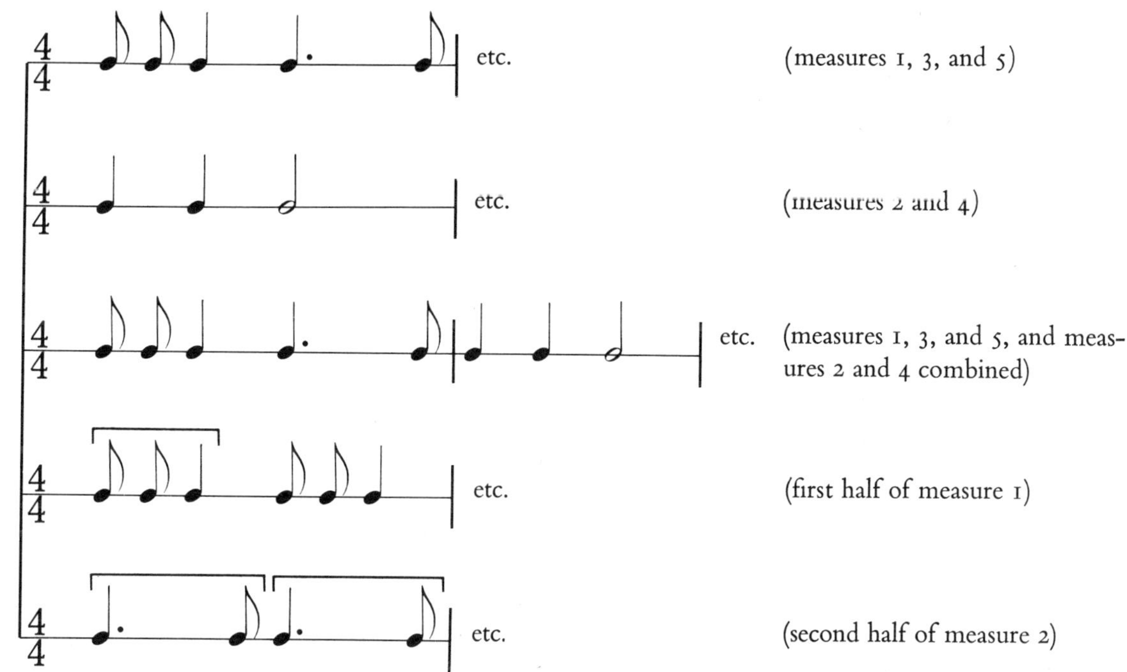
etc.
(measures 1, 3, and 5)
etc.
(measures 2 and 4)
etc.
(measures 1, 3, and 5, and measures 2 and 4 combined)
etc.
(first half of measure 1)
etc.
(second half of measure 2)

Example 2: OVER THE RIVER AND THROUGH THE WOOD

1 2 3 4 5
O - ver the ri - ver and through the wood, To Grand-fa - ther's house we go; The horse knows the way to
6 7 8 9 10
car - ry the sleigh, Through the white and drift - ed snow. O - ver the ri - ver and through the wood, Oh,
11 12 13 14 15 16
how the wind does blow, It stings the toes, and bites the nose, as o - ver the ground we go.

SUMMARY

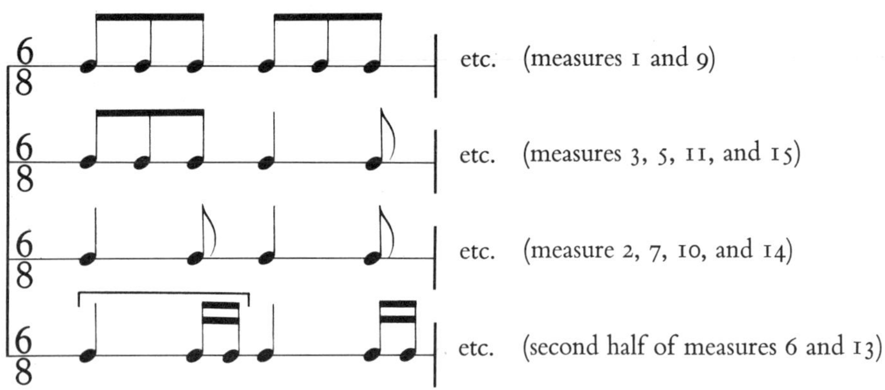
etc. (measures 1 and 9)
etc. (measures 3, 5, 11, and 15)
etc. (measure 2, 7, 10, and 14)
etc. (second half of measures 6 and 13)

Example 3: TEN LITTLE INDIANS

1
2
3
4
One lit - tle, two lit - tle, three lit - tle In - dians, Four lit - tle, five lit - tle, six lit - tle In - dians,
5
6
7
8
Seven lit - tle, eight lit - tle, nine lit - tle In - dians, Ten lit - tle In - dian boys.

SUMMARY

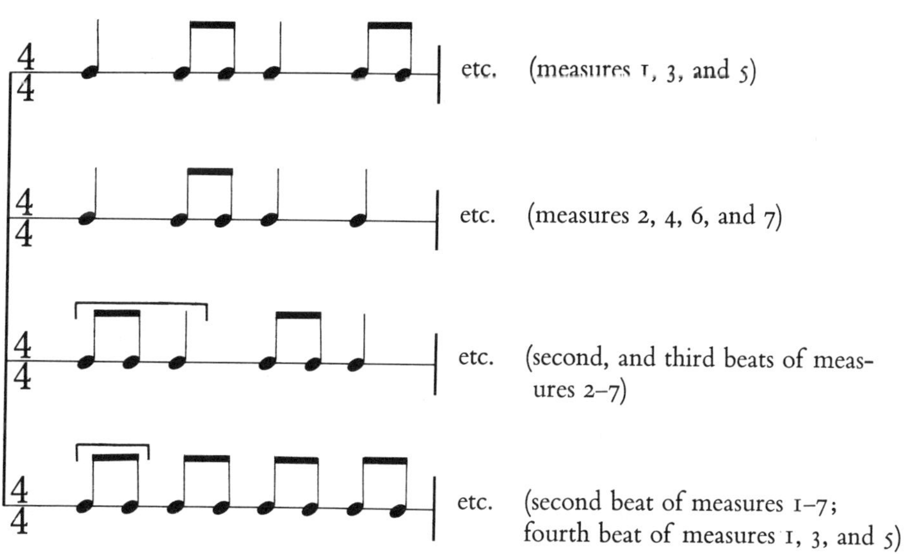
etc. (measures 1, 3, and 5)
etc. (measures 2, 4, 6, and 7)
etc. (second, and third beats of measures 2–7)
etc. (second beat of measures 1–7; fourth beat of measures 1, 3, and 5)

Example 4: THIS OLD MAN

1
2
3
4
5
6
This old man, he played one, He played nick-nack on my thumb, With a nick-nack pad-dy whack, give the dog a bone,

7
8
This old man came roll - ing home.

SUMMARY

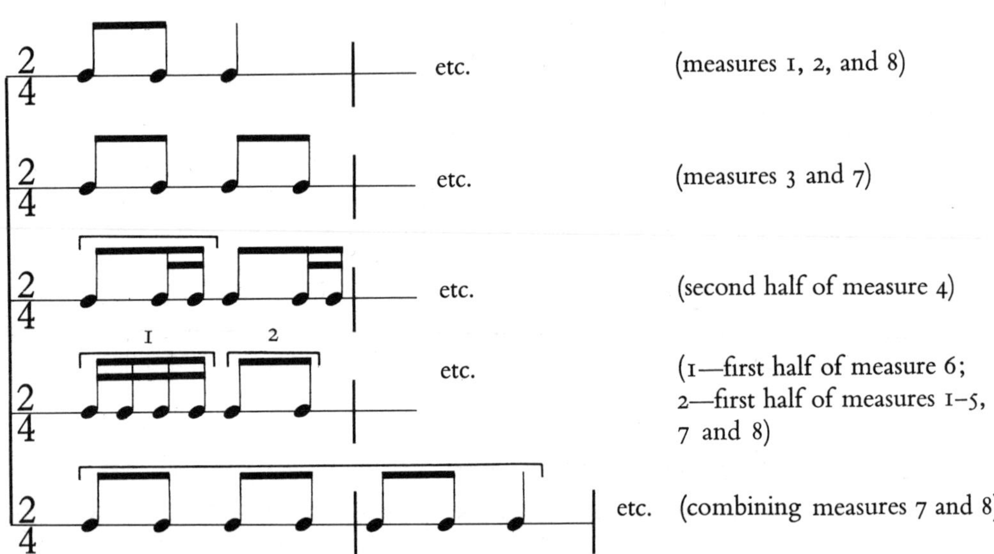
etc. (measures 1, 2, and 8)
etc. (measures 3 and 7)
etc. (second half of measure 4)
1
2
etc. (1—first half of measure 6; 2—first half of measures 1–5, 7 and 8)
etc. (combining measures 7 and 8)

Example 5: AMERICA

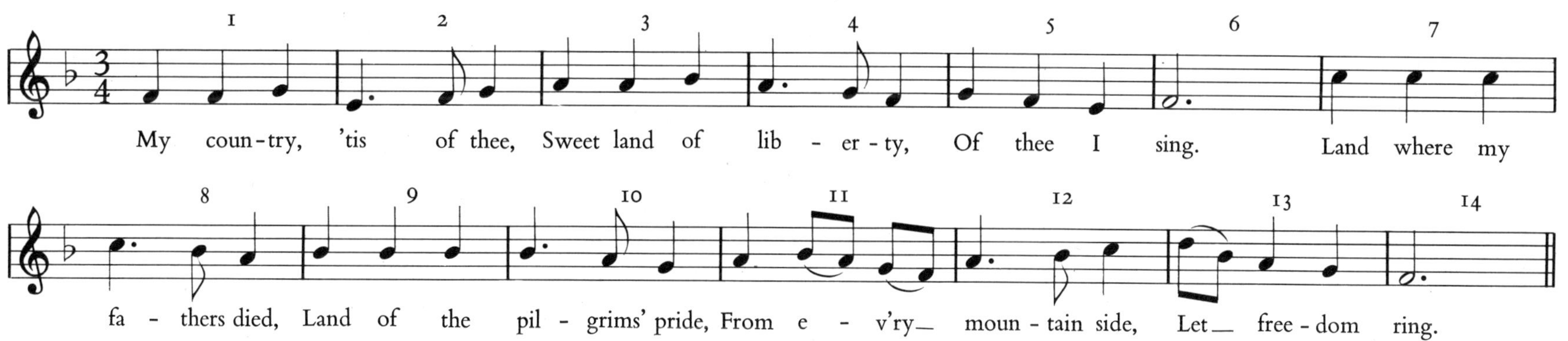
1 2 3 4 5 6 7
My coun-try, 'tis of thee, Sweet land of lib - er - ty, Of thee I sing. Land where my
8 9 10 11 12 13 14
fa - thers died, Land of the pil - grims' pride, From e - v'ry— moun - tain side, Let— free - dom ring.

SUMMARY

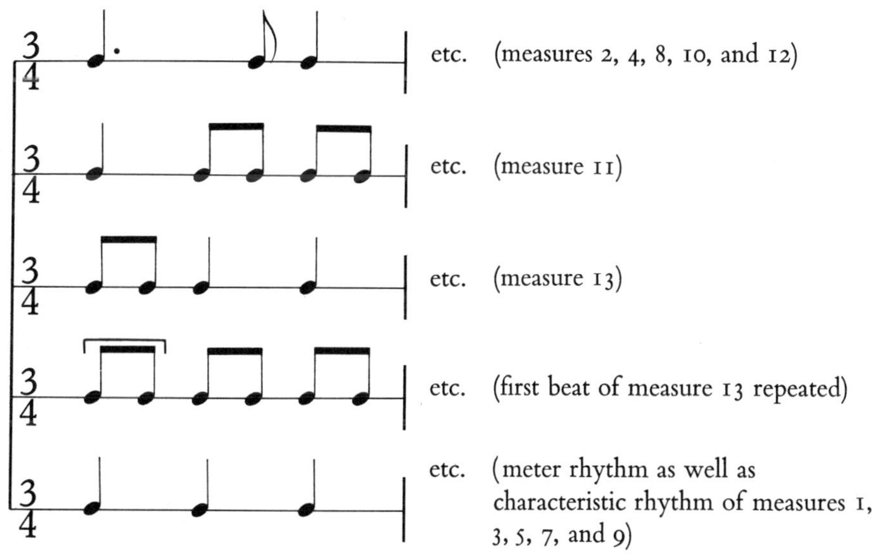
etc. (measures 2, 4, 8, 10, and 12)
etc. (measure 11)
etc. (measure 13)
etc. (first beat of measure 13 repeated)
etc. (meter rhythm as well as characteristic rhythm of measures 1, 3, 5, 7, and 9)

Example 6: ALOUETTE

1
2
3
4
Fine
5
A - lou-et - te, gen-tille a - lou-et - te, A - lou-et - te, je te plu-me-rai. Je te plu - me-rai la tête,
6
7
8
D.C. al Fine
Je te plu-me-rai la tête, Et la tête, et la tête. Oh!

SUMMARY

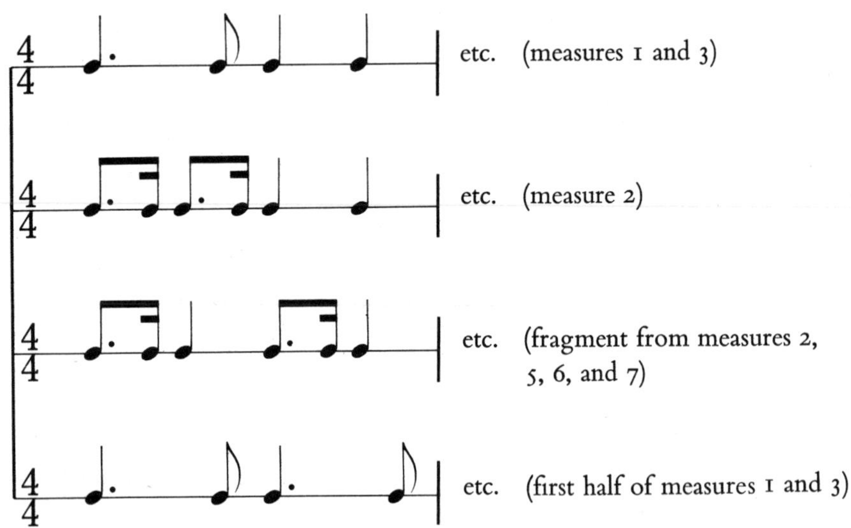
etc. (measures 1 and 3)
etc. (measure 2)
etc. (fragment from measures 2, 5, 6, and 7)
etc. (first half of measures 1 and 3)

Example 7: SANTA LUCIA

1 2 3 4 5 6 7 8
Now 'neath the sil-ver moon, O - cean is glow - ing, O'er the calm bil - low, Soft winds are blow-ing.
9 10 11 12 13 14 15 16
Here balm - y breez-es blow, Pure joys in - vite__ us, And as we gent-ly row, All things de - light us.

SUMMARY

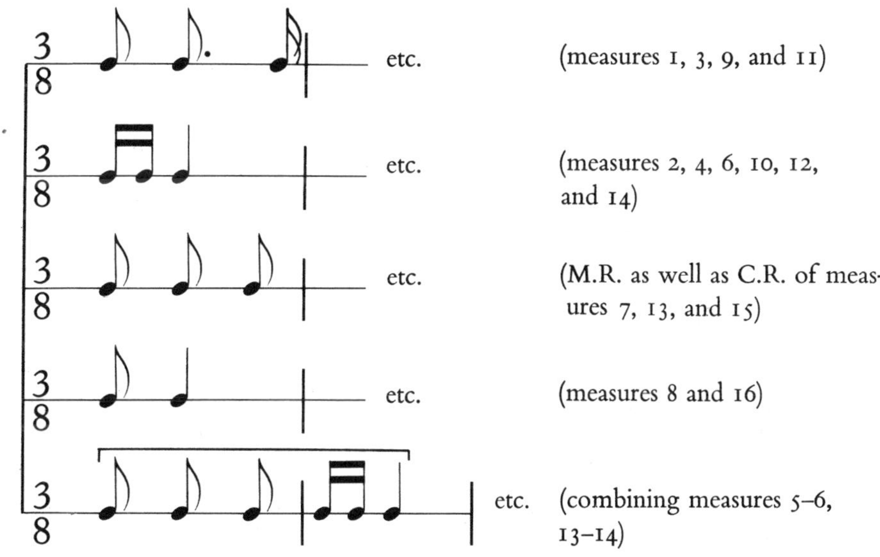
etc.
(measures 1, 3, 9, and 11)
etc.
(measures 2, 4, 6, 10, 12, and 14)
etc.
(M.R. as well as C.R. of measures 7, 13, and 15)
etc.
(measures 8 and 16)
etc.
(combining measures 5–6, 13–14)

3 Reference List of Rhythm Patterns

In addition to rhythmic patterns structured from meter rhythms and characteristic rhythms found in an original melody, there is other source material on which the student may improvise when scoring rhythmic activities. Following is a compilation of various rhythmic patterns that are typical of music written in the three meters from which most other meters evolve. These typical patterns occur with high frequency in music literature for children.

4
4
3
4
6
8

The ability to improvise on these patterns, on the M.R., and on the C.R. is the ultimate goal of the *creative* aspect of this activity. Though the above compilation is in no way considered to be exhaustive, it does provide representative rhythmic pattern types likely to be found in music literature for elementary age children. Many of these will be identical with the M.R. or the C.R.

Many children's pieces will be so structured melodically that little rhythmic activity can be found to provide a suitable rhythmic orchestration. In these instances, the student should use one or more of the above patterns. As the student develops her skill, she will consider seriously the possibility of interpolating many of these rhythm patterns with those which are characteristic of the melody.

B. Procedure for Orchestrating Rhythmic Activities

The teacher will need to decide how much rhythmic activity and how many rhythm instruments are desired for a given situation. Since different melodies have different melodic and rhythmic characteristics, predetermining an exact number of rhythmic activities and a definite, fixed instrumentation for all melodies would be neither feasible nor practical. From a music education point of view, children should have an opportunity to develop as many rhythmic skills as possible. It should be remembered that these rhythmic skills will aid in future musical experiences. With an actual performance goal in mind, however, it may be that a limited number of patterns would be most satisfactory. For purposes of practice in the evolvement of rhythmic patterns and to afford ample opportunities for students to experiment with various instrumental combinations, the procedure in this study will be to orchestrate for *three* rhythmic activities only.

There are many kinds of percussion instruments, and the characteristics of each should be kept in mind when orchestrating for these instruments. Decisions will have to be made as to which instruments produce the most appropriate sound effects and which will be most compatible with the different types of rhythmic patterns found in existing melodies. For example, smaller, lighter instruments will best be scored to play faster, more intricate types of rhythmic patterns, while the larger instruments will best be scored to play the basic beats and accents. Instruments that ring are suitable to enhance gay, light, and higher pitched music. Drums and other larger instruments provide good background for deep and low sounding music. No definite, unalterable instrumentation is projected in this study since it is believed that only through repeated experimentation will real creative rhythmic orchestration result.

GROUPINGS OF REPRESENTATIVE
RHYTHM INSTRUMENTS

Type I.
Scored to play light, clicking, fast patterns.

Rhythm Sticks
Wood Blocks
Tone Blocks
Claves
Castanets

Type II.
Scored to produce a ringing or clanging effect.

Cymbals
Wrist Bells*
Triangles
Tambourines*
Jingle Sticks*

Type III.
Scored to produce a "brushed" and partially sustained effect.

Sand Blocks
Maracas and other shakers

Type IV.
Scored to establish the fundamental "beat."

Drums

* If these are shaken, they can be used to produce sustained sounds.

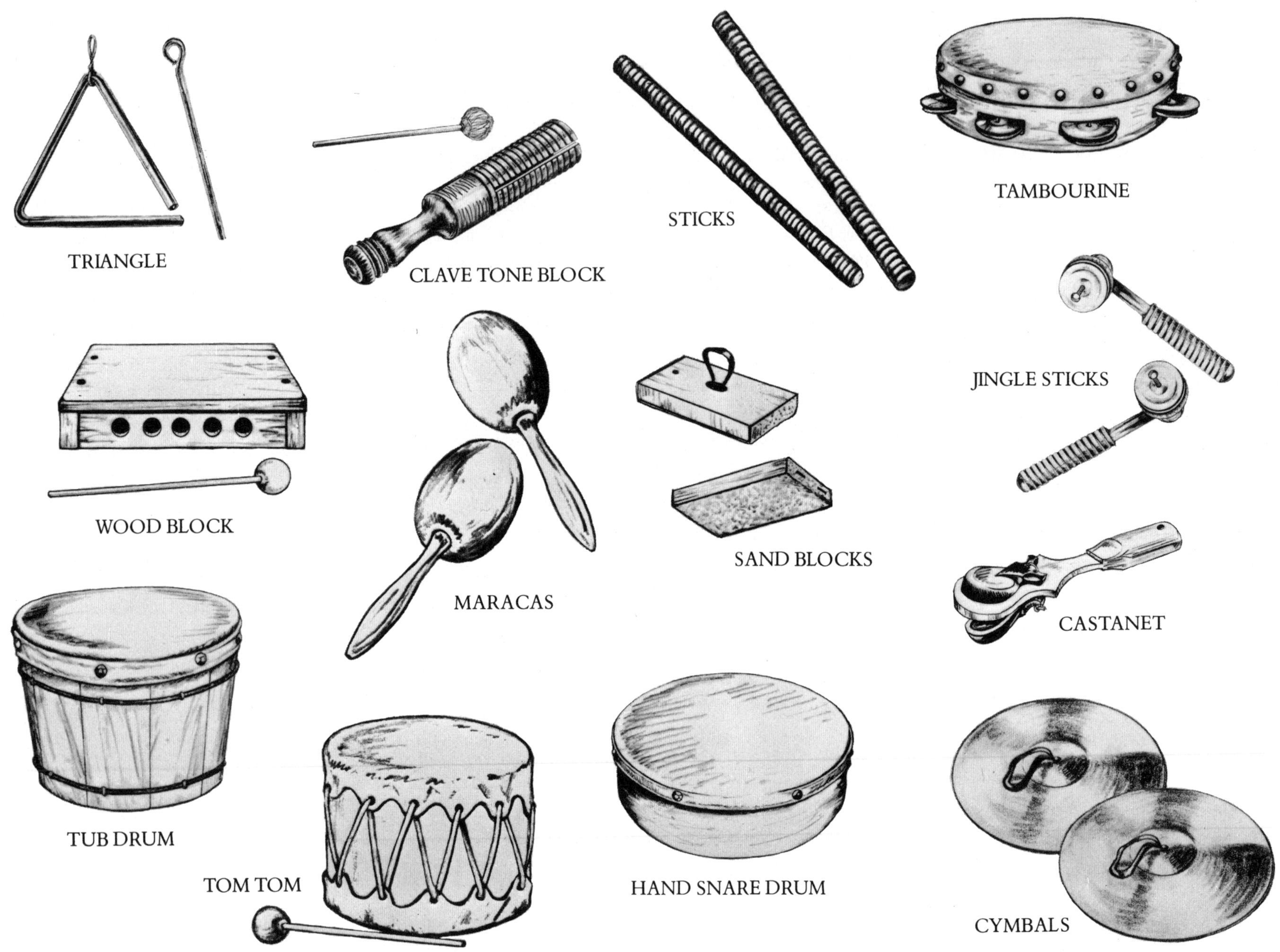
TRIANGLE
CLAVE TONE BLOCK
STICKS
TAMBOURINE
JINGLE STICKS
WOOD BLOCK
MARACAS
SAND BLOCKS
CASTANET
TUB DRUM
TOM TOM
HAND SNARE DRUM
CYMBALS

A selected group of percussion instruments which can be used in the elementary classroom.

The following example, "This Old Man," is used to illustrate a typical step-by-step procedure for *orchestrating rhythmic activities:*

STEP 1. Find the *meter rhythm.* The meter of this melody is $\frac{2}{4}$. The meter rhythm, then, will be scored as two quarter notes per measure. Repeat the quarter note pattern throughout the entire melody.

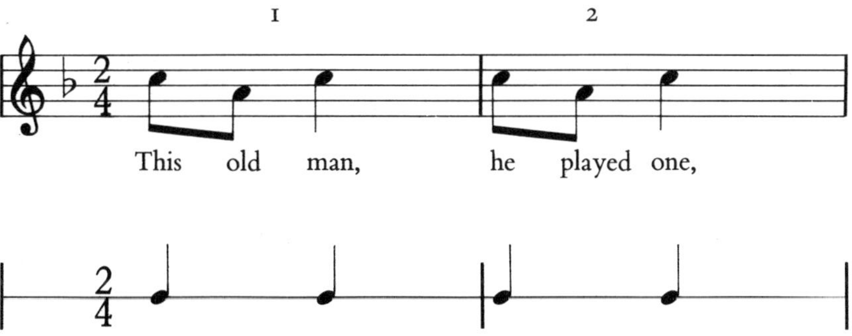
1
2
This old man, he played one,

NOTE: All rhythmic patterns should be scored so as to be "lined up" in accurate relation to basic pulsations and subdivisions.

STEP 2. Find the main *characteristic rhythm.* If one searches through the melody, it becomes obvious that the two eighth notes and one quarter note found in measure 1 and then in measures 2 and 8 are "characteristic" of the melodic line. This pattern, which consumes one measure, should be notated throughout the piece.

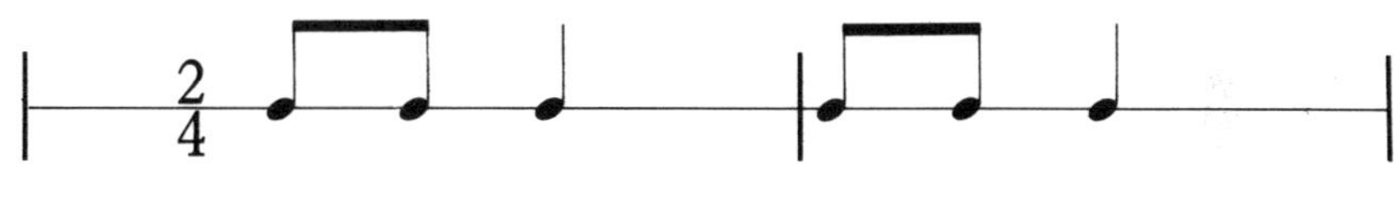

STEP 3. Find other characteristic rhythms that consume whole measures. Used less frequently, but still very characteristic both of this melody and of $\frac{2}{4}$ meter in general, are the four eighth notes which are found in measures 3 and 7 and which provide an exciting rhythmic activity. Repeat this measure throughout the piece.

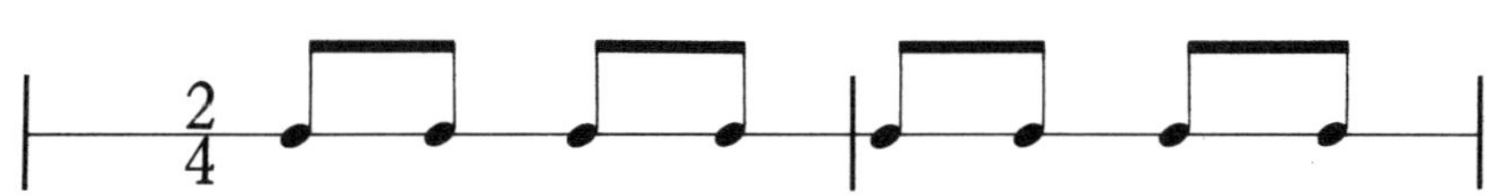

Now, three different rhythmic activities have been evolved, or created, from this tune. Without going any further, this would be sufficient for activity involving percussion instruments. However, each tune should be studied and analyzed to determine what additional patterns might be structured. As more and more proficiency and skill are developed, these "extra" patterns could be orchestrated to good advantage.

STEP 4. Seek additional rhythmic patterns. All the previous patterns have consumed entire measures. At this point, we should look for those patterns which are typical, or characteristic, but do not occupy an entire measure. A good example is the first half of measure 6—four sixteenth notes. By repeating these four notes, a measure of eight sixteenth notes is created.

STEP 5. Still another pattern which seems quite characteristic is found in the last half of measure 4, one eighth and two sixteenth notes.

3 4 5 6 7 8
He played nick-nack on my thumb, With a nick-nack pad-dy whack, give the dog a bone, This old man came roll-ing home.

SUMMARY

Following is a completed orchestration of rhythmic activities utilizing all five patterns evolved from the original melody. The student will need to determine just which three of these would be most practical for classroom use. It is advised that during the several-step procedure the student seek to create as many patterns as she possibly can. It is quite possible that, at one time or another, she may wish to use all the patterns.

Melody
1
2
3
4
This old man, he played one, He played nick - nack on my thumb, With a
Step 1
Step 2
Step 3
Step 4
Step 5

5 6 7 8

nick - nack pad-dy whack, give the dog a bone, This old man came roll - ing home.

It should be remembered that the composite sound of the measures above (take measure 1, for example) would be: 
This is actually the sound that the ear would hear when the different rhythm patterns are played together. Although you would be hearing different instruments playing a different number of notes, the end result would still actually be this sound.

This should be kept in mind when structuring rhythmic patterns and designating instruments to be used. If a tub drum were scored for C.R. 3 in measure 1, the lighter instruments playing the other rhythmic patterns would be drowned out. Make sure that the lighter instruments can be heard.

The fact must not be overlooked that *rests* play a very real part in rhythmic activities. It is important that children become familiar with rests and their purpose in music. The song previously analyzed and orchestrated is shown below, but this time it has been scored to utilize rests as part of the rhythmic activity. By participating in this type of activity, the children will become experienced in playing their instruments at certain times, resting while other instruments or group of instruments play, and then coming back in with their own instruments.

1
2
3
4
Melody
This old man, he played one, He played nick - nack on my thumb, With a
M.R.:
HAND SNARE DRUM
C.R. 1:
CLAVES
C.R. 2:
TRIANGLE
C.R. 3:
STICKS
C.R. 4:
TAMBOURINE

5
6
7
8
nick - nack pad-dy whack, give the dog a bone, This old man came roll - ing home.

2 Application

A. Composed Throughout

COMPOSED THROUGHOUT is a term used to indicate that the rhythmic patterns selected as meter rhythm and the two characteristic rhythms are scored in repetition throughout the entire selection. By studying the following examples, students will observe the correct procedure for notating rhythmic patterns so that they "line up" according to the basic pulsations and subdivisions.

TEN LITTLE INDIANS
United States
Melody
One lit - tle, two lit - tle, three lit - tle In - dians, Four lit - tle, five lit - tle, six lit - tle In - dians,
M.R.:
TOM TOM DRUM, TAMBOURINE
C.R. 1:
CLAVES, STICKS
C.R. 2:
WOOD BLOCKS, TRIANGLE

Seven lit - tle, eight lit - tle, nine lit - tle In - dians, Ten lit - tle In - dian boys.

LAVENDER'S BLUE

England

Melody
Lav - en - der's blue, dil - ly dil - ly, Lav - en - der's green; When I am
M.R.:
TAMBOURINE, WOOD BLOCKS
C.R. 1:
CLAVES, STICKS
C.R. 2:
DRUMS, CYMBALS

king, dil - ly dil - ly, you shall be queen.

WHITE CORAL BELLS

England

Melody
White co - ral bells up - on a slen-der stalk, Lil - ies of the val-ley deck my gar - den walk.
M.R.:
TUB DRUM
C.R. 1:
STICKS
C.R. 2:
WRIST BELLS, TRIANGLE

THERE WAS A CROOKED MAN

Nursery Tune

Melody
There was a crook - ed man, and he walked a crook - ed mile, He
M.R.:
HAND SNARE DRUM
C.R. 1:
JINGLE STICKS
C.R. 2:
SAND BLOCKS

found a crook-ed six - pence up - on a crook-ed stile, He bought a crook-ed cat, which

caught a crook-ed mouse, And they all lived to-geth-er in a crook-ed lit-tle house.

B. Improvised Rhythms

IMPROVISED RHYTHMS is a term used to indicate that freedom and flexibility are permitted in the evolvement, or creation, of rhythmic orchestrations. The following examples, which make use of rests and special sound effects, reveal this to a degree.

THE PAPAYA TREE

Philippines

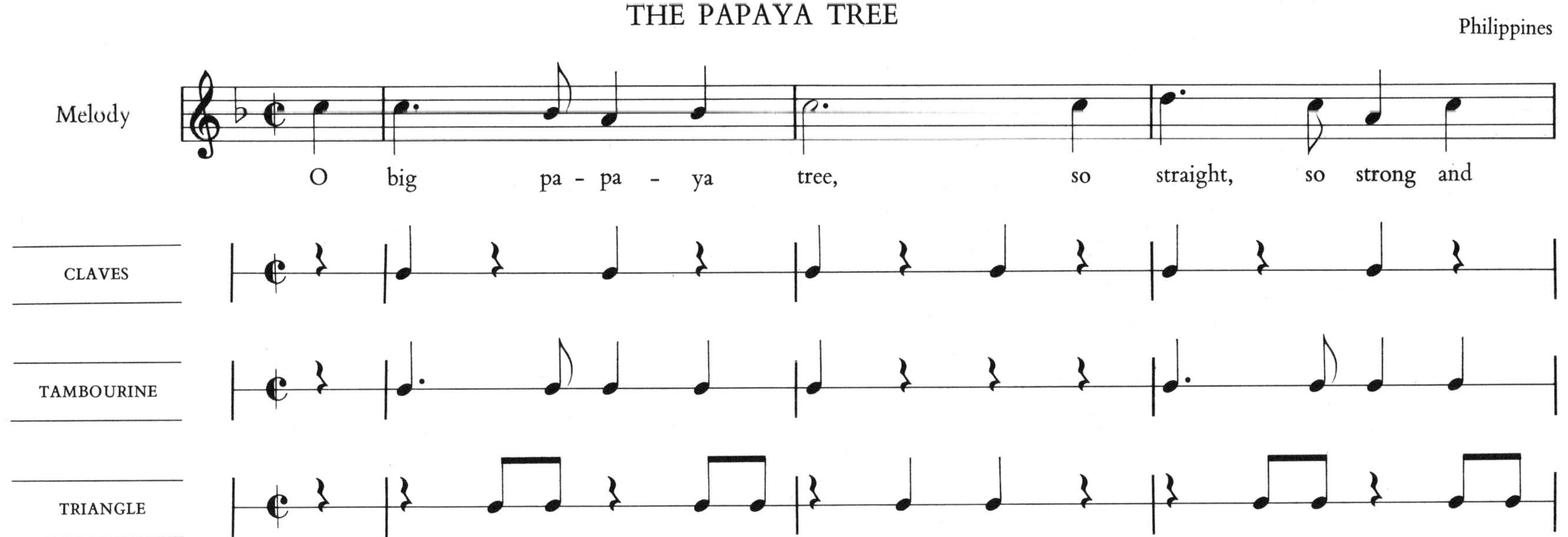
Melody
O big pa-pa-ya tree, so straight, so strong and
CLAVES
TAMBOURINE
TRIANGLE

high; A mes - sage take for me far up in - to the
sky. Please tell the glow - ing sun we thank him for his

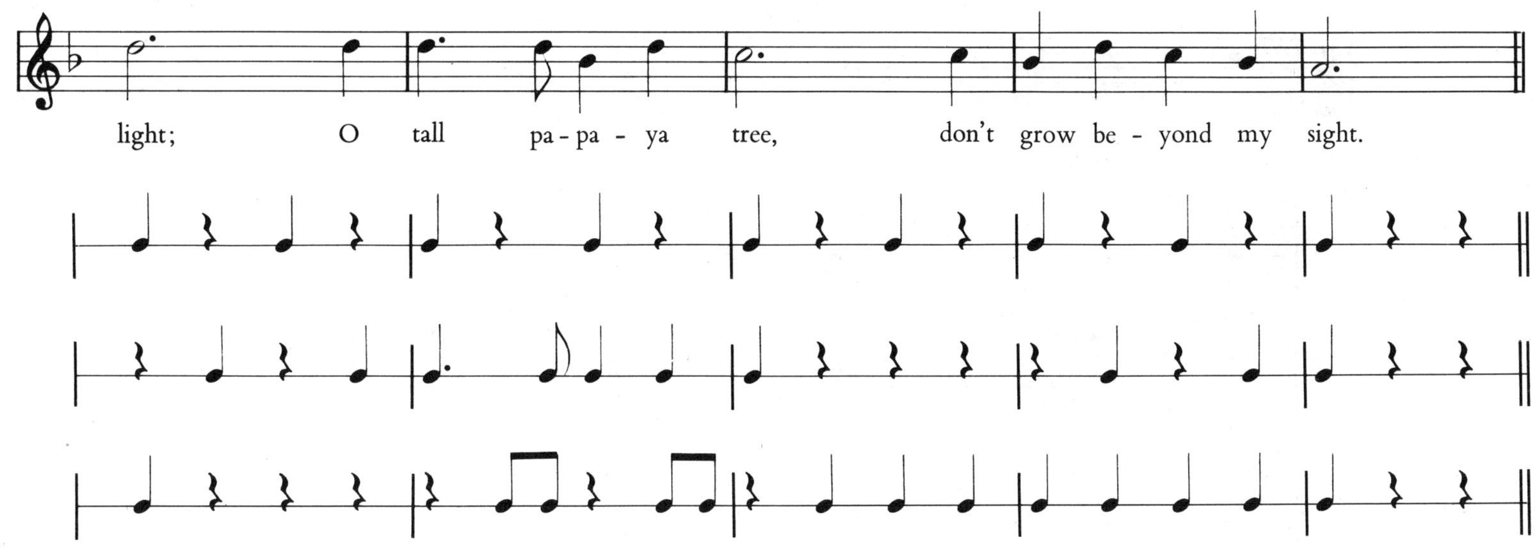
light; O tall pa - pa - ya tree, don't grow be - yond my sight.

LAS POLLITAS

(The Little Chickens)

Spanish Folk Song

Melody
Pin - ti - tas de co - lo - ra - do, Son las pol - li - tas que ten - go, Pin -
RHYTHM STICKS
CASTANETS
TAMBOURINE
hit shake shake

ti - tas de co - lo - ra - do, Son las pol - li - tas que ten - go, Pero
est - a - ca - pe - ton ci - ta No la ven - do no la ven - do, Pero

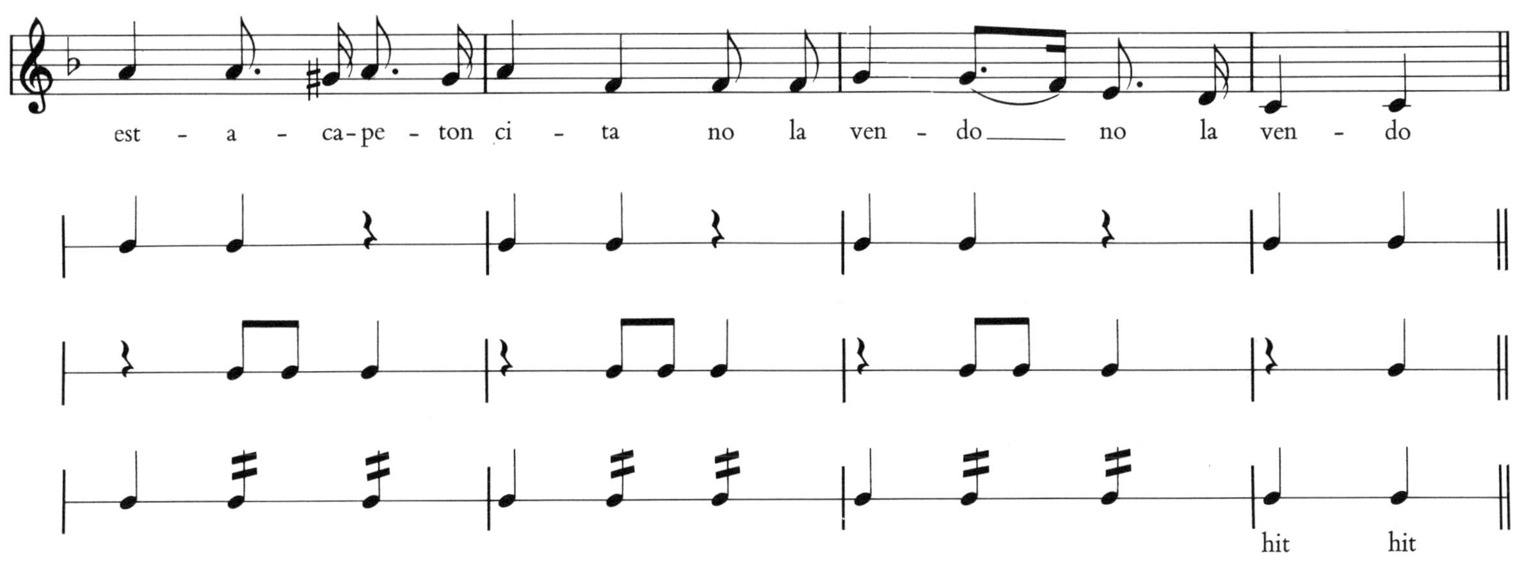
est - a - ca-pe - ton ci - ta no la ven - do no la ven - do
hit hit

YANKEE DOODLE

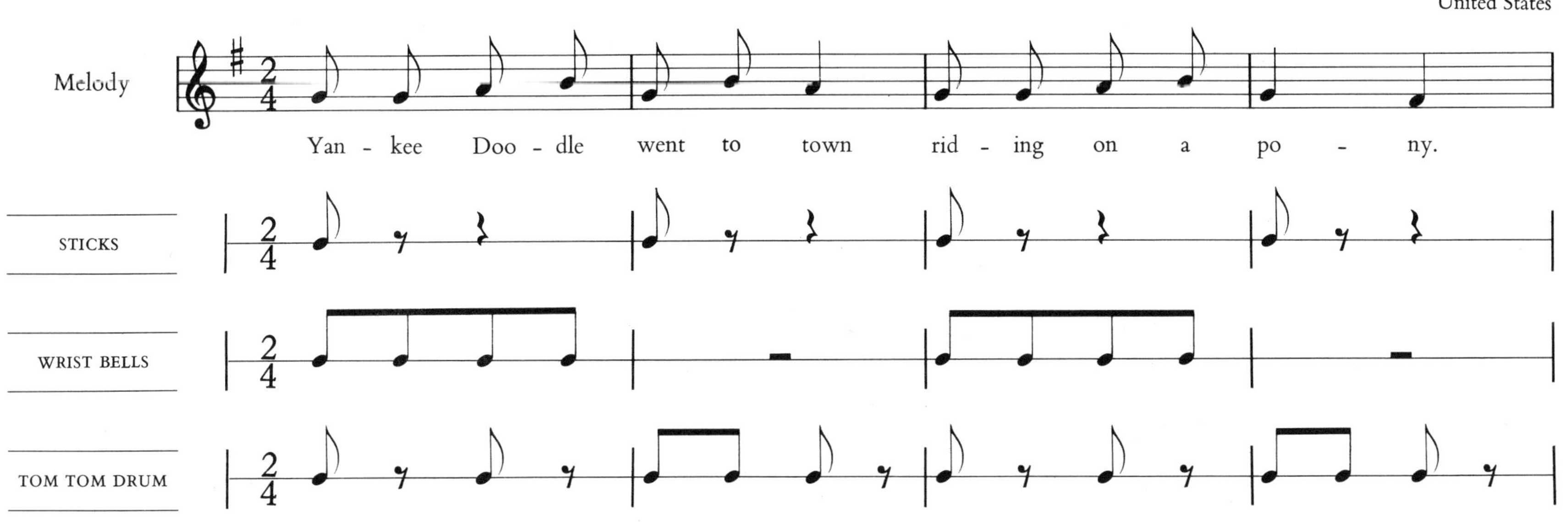
United States
Melody
Yan - kee Doo - dle went to town rid - ing on a po - ny.
STICKS
WRIST BELLS
TOM TOM DRUM

Stuck a fea - ther in his hat and called it ma - ca - ro - ni.

OATS, PEAS, BEANS

England

Melody
Oats, peas, beans, and bar - ley grow; Oats, peas, beans, and bar - ley grow; Do
TAMBOURINE
s
shake
hit — —
HAND SNARE DRUM
TRIANGLE

you or I or an - y - one know, How oats, peas, beans, and bar - ley grow?
S
S

3 Assignments: Student Worksheets

It is suggested that the student first structure rhythmic activities on a rough copy of manuscript paper. When the orchestration has been completed, she should transfer the material to sheets provided in this workbook. Before beginning the rough draft, she should carefully study the examples for ideas.

The worksheets are also divided into two groups:

A. *Composed Throughout:* This group of worksheets provides percussion staves upon which the student is to structure (a) *meter rhythm*, (b) *C.R.1*, (c) *C.R.2*. The arbitrary limitation of rhythmic activities to three instruments, or groups of instruments, should be of no concern to the student at this point. It is felt that this number will be sufficient until more experience and skill have been obtained.

For this group, structure the rhythmic activities throughout the entire section. Also, be certain to designate the instrument(s) which is to perform each percussion score.

B. *Improvised Rhythms:* This group of worksheets is also prepared with three percussion staves. However, here the student is to assume greater freedom and flexibility in structuring the rhythmic activities. The use of rests and rhythmic patterns derived from portions of a measure, from the combination of two or more measures of the original melody, and/or from the reference list of rhythmic patterns of the student's own choosing provide the basis for this freedom.

This group of songs should begin to reflect clearly the concept of *orchestration*, the basic premise upon which this book has been conceived.

Blank manuscript paper is included at the end of each group for the student to do additional rhythmic orchestrations. The selection of the music material to be used is left to the discretion of the instructor and/or student. At the end of each part of the book there is a perforated sheet (divided into four sections) which is included for the purpose of showing how individual parts can be structured so members of the class can perform assigned selections. Need for additional parts will require the student to construct her own manuscript paper for this purpose.

A. Composed Throughout

Name ______________________________

SKIP TO MY LOU

United States
Melody
1 2 3 4
Lou, Lou, skip to my Lou, Lou, Lou, skip to my Lou,
M.R.:
C.R. 1:
C.R. 2:
5 6 7 8
Lou, Lou, skip to my Lou, Skip to my Lou, my dar - ling.

Name ____________________

ARE YOU SLEEPING?

France

Melody
1
2
3
4
Are you sleep - ing, are you sleep - ing, Broth - er John, Broth - er John?
M.R.:
C.R. 1:
C.R. 2:
5
6
7
8
Morn-ing bells are ring - ing, morn-ing bells are ring - ing, Ding ding dong, ding ding dong.

Name ______________________________

BOW BELINDA

United States
Melody
1 2 3 4
Bow, bow, bow Be - lin - da; Bow, bow, bow Be - lin - da;
M.R.:
C.R. 1:
C.R. 2:
5 6 7 8
Bow, bow, bow Be - lin - da; Won't you be my dar - ling?

Name ______________________________

ROW, ROW, ROW, YOUR BOAT

Round
Melody
1 2 3 4
Row row row your boat, Gent - ly down the stream.
M.R.:
C.R. 1:
C.R. 2:
5 6 7 8
Mer - ri - ly mer - ri - ly mer - ri - ly mer - ri - ly, Life is but a dream.

Name ______________________

BICYCLE BUILT FOR TWO

Harry Dacre
Melody
1 2 3 4 5 6
Dai - - - sy, Dai - - - sy, Give me your an - swer
M.R.:
C.R. 1:
C.R. 2:
7 8 9 10 11 12 13
true. I'm half cra - - - zy, All for the

14
15
16
17
18
19
20
love of you. It won't be a sty - lish mar - riage, I
21
22
23
24
25
26
can't af - ford a car - riage. But you'll look sweet

27
28
29
30
31
32
on the seat of a bi - cy - cle built for two.

Name ______________________________

PUSSY CAT

J. W. Elliott

Melody

Pus - sy cat, pus - sy cat, where have you been? "I've been to Lon-don to vis - it the queen."

M.R.: ____________

____

C.R. 1: ____________

____

C.R. 2: ____________

____

Pus - sy cat, pus - sy cat, what did you there? "I fright-ened a lit - tle mouse un - der her chair."

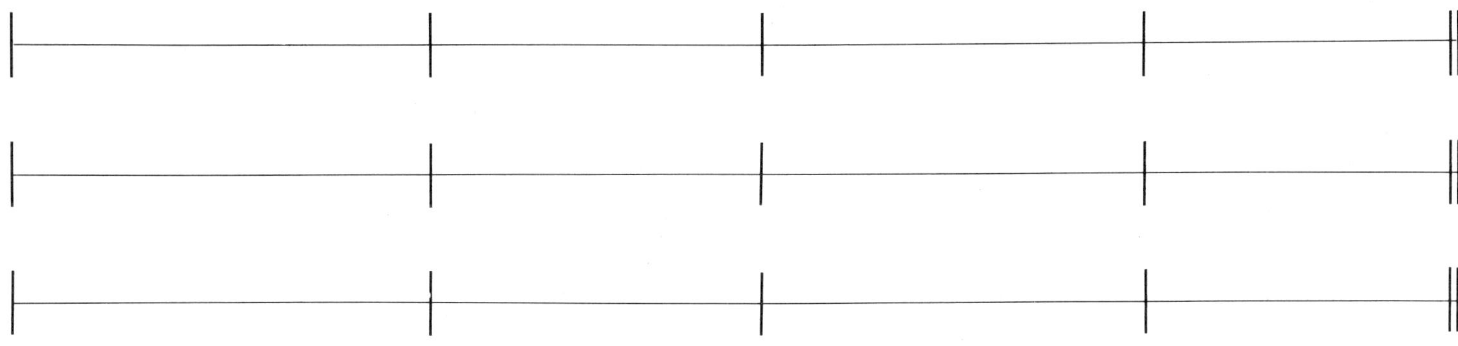

Name ____________________

MY HOME'S IN MONTANA

Cowboy Song
Melody
My home's in Mon ta - na, I wear a ban - dan - a, My
M.R.:
C.R. 1:
C.R. 2:
spurs are of sil - ver, My pon - - y is gray; When

rid - ing the ran - ges, My luck ne - ver chan - ges, With
foot in the stir - rup I gal - lop a - way.

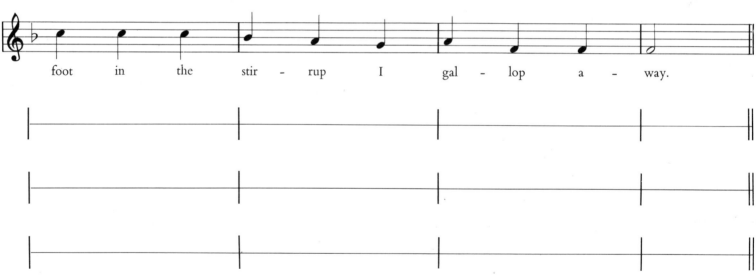

Name ______________________________

Melody

M.R.:

C.R. 1:

C.R. 2:

Name ______________________

Melody

M.R.:

C.R. 1:

C.R. 2:

Name ______________________

Melody

M.R.:

C.R. 1:

C.R. 2:

Name ______________________________

Melody

M.R.:

C.R. I:

C.R. 2:

Name ______________________

Melody

M.R.:

C.R. 1:

C.R. 2:

Name ______________________________

Melody

M.R.:

C.R. 1:

C.R. 2:

Name ____________________

Melody

M.R.:

C.R. 1:

C.R. 2:

Name ____________________

Melody

M.R.:

C.R. 1:

C.R. 2:

Name ______________________

Melody

M.R.: ______

C.R. 1: ______

C.R. 2: ______

Name ______________________________

Melody

M.R.:

C.R. 1:

C.R. 2:

B. Improvised Rhythms

Name ______________________

THE SLEEPING PRINCESS
Sweden
Melody
1
2
3
4
There was a pret - ty prin - cess, a prin - cess, a prin - cess, There
5
6
7
8
was a pret - ty prin - cess long a - go!

Name ______________________

COCKLES AND MUSSELS

Ireland
Melody
In Dub - lin's fair cit - y, Where girls are so pret - ty, I
first set my eyes on sweet Mol - ly Ma - lone, As she

9
10
11
12
wheeled her wheel - bar - row, Through streets broad and nar - row, Cry - ing,
13
14
15
16
"Cock - les and mus - sels, a - live, a - live oh!"

Name ____________________

THE QUAKER'S WIFE

Scotland
Melody
1 2 3 4
The Quak - er's wife sat down to bake, With all her bairns a - bout her. She
5 6 7 8
made them all a sug - ar cake, And the mil - ler wants his mout - er.

Chorus
9
10
11
12
Mer - ri - ly danced the Quak - er's wife, And mer - ri - ly danced the Quak - er;
13
14
15
16
Mer - ri - ly danced the Quak - er's wife, And mer - ri - ly danced the Quak - er.

Name ______________________

WHAT SHALL WE DO ON A RAINY DAY?

Old Tune

Melody

What shall we do on a rain - y day, rain - y day, rain - y day?

What shall we do on a rain - y day when we can't go out to play?

Name ______________________

WALK ALONG, JOHN

Oklahoma

Melody
Come on boys and hush your talk - ing, All join hands and
let's go walk - ing. Walk a - long, John, with your pa - per col - lar on.

Name ______________________

PONY SONG

Germany
Melody
Hop, hop, hop, Go and nev - er stop.
When it's smooth and when it's ston - y, Go a - long my lit - tle pon - y,

Go and nev - er stop.
Hop, hop, hop, hop, hop.

Name ______________________

SONGS MY MOTHER TAUGHT ME

Anton Dvořák

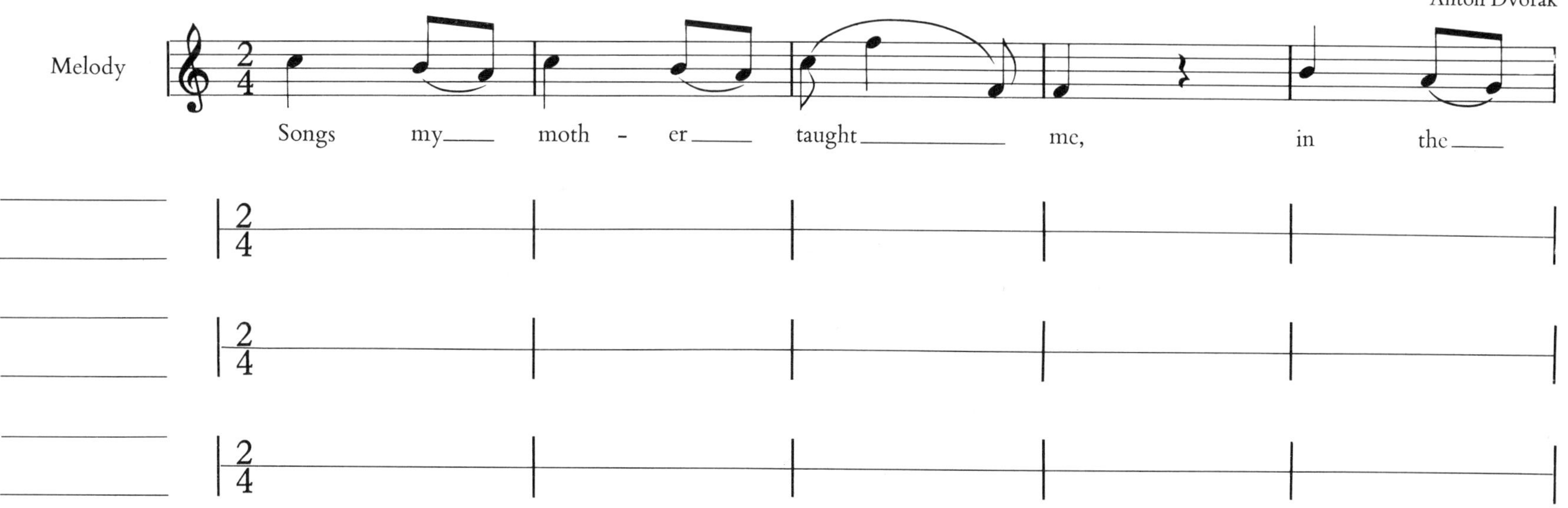
Melody
Songs my moth - er taught me, in the

days long van - - - ished; Sel - - dom from her

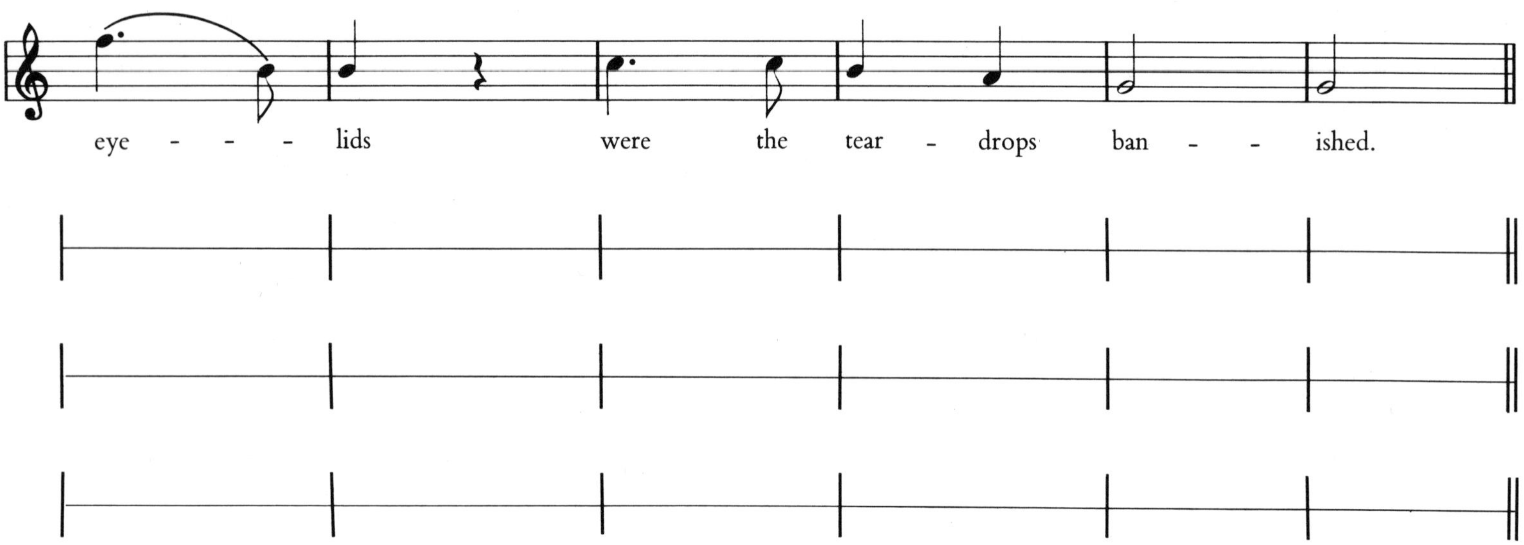
eye - - - lids were the tear - drops ban - - ished.

Name ______________________________

Name ______________________________

Name ______________________________

Name ______________________________

Name ______________________________

Name ______________________________

Name ______________________________

Name ______________________________

Name ________________________________

(name of selection)

(instrument)

(name of selection)

(instrument)

(name of selection)

(instrument)

(name of selection)

(instrument)

(name of selection)

(instrument)

(name of selection)

(instrument)

(name of selection)

(instrument)

(name of selection)

(instrument)

(name of selection)

(instrument)

(name of selection)

(instrument)

(name of selection)

(instrument)

(name of selection)

(instrument)

(name of selection)

(instrument)

(name of selection)

(instrument)

(name of selection)

(instrument)

(name of selection)

(instrument)

(name of selection)

(instrument)

(name of selection)

(instrument)

(name of selection)

(instrument)

(name of selection)

(instrument)

Part 2

MELODY

I Theory and Analysis

The purpose of this part is to teach the procedure for creating one or more melodies from an existing melody. These additional melodic lines are referred to as *descarts*, or melody 1, melody 2, etc. Our source here, just as in the case of rhythm, is the *original* melody. The number of melodies that a student may wish to compose will depend largely on practical usage and need. A step-by-step procedure for evolving these additions is discussed below.

It is suggested that the student constantly keep in mind that the ultimate goal of music education in the classroom is to provide as many musical activities for the children as possible. Involvement of young instrumentalists in performing descants on their instruments is extremely sound motivation. Besides utilizing melody instruments traditionally used in elementary classrooms, pupils studying a wind or string instrument in the local instrumental program of the school should be given opportunities to further their performing skills. For example, should there be a pupil studying clarinet, include this child in the performance of one of the newly created melodic lines. Further, periodic division of the class into vocal, melody, and rhythm performing sections results in highly successful musical experiences. The main purpose is the realization of a truly "orchestral" experience for the children.

A. Definition of Terms

1. Primary Harmonies

PRIMARY HARMONIES are chords built on the first, fourth, and fifth degrees of the scale. These chords are referred to as TONIC (I), SUBDOMINANT (IV), and DOMINANT (V). The DOMINANT SEVEN (V_7) is usually used instead of the DOMINANT (V) in order to obtain a fuller, more complete sound. This is accomplished by adding another note a third above the top note of the DOMINANT (V), as shown below:

Example 1: C Major

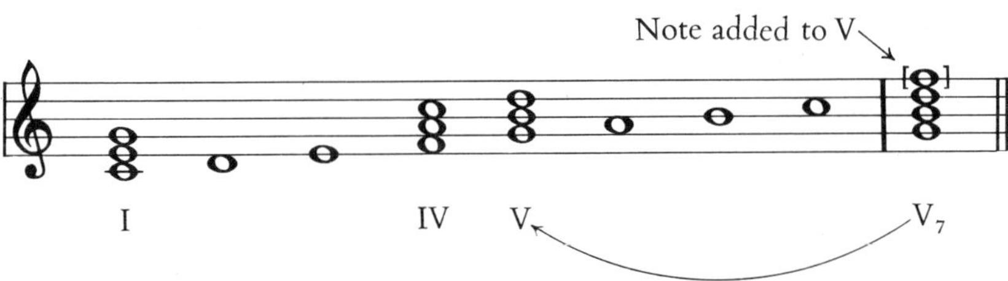

Note added to V
I
IV
V
V_7

Throughout this section, the V_7 will be used instead of the V.

For *playing position* some notes are moved (inverted) so that the chords will be more convenient to play on the keyboard. In the *subdominant* the C is taken and moved down an octave below. The notes are still F A C but have been rearranged so that the hand has to make very little movement in going from the Tonic (I) to the *subdominant* (IV). In the V_7, the root of the chord, G, is left in place and the other notes are moved down below it. The following illustration shows the *tonic* (I), *subdominant* (IV), and *dominant seventh* (V_7) for the key of C major in playing position.

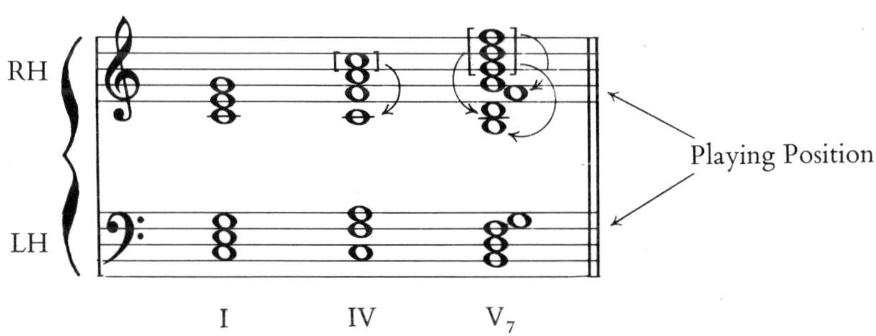

RH
LH
Playing Position
I
IV
V_7

Playing positions in other keys, arranged in this same manner, are shown in the examples that follow.

NOTE: In the balance of this book, the fifth of the V_7 chord is omitted in order to provide a smoother connection between chords preceding and following it.

Example 2: A Harmonic Minor

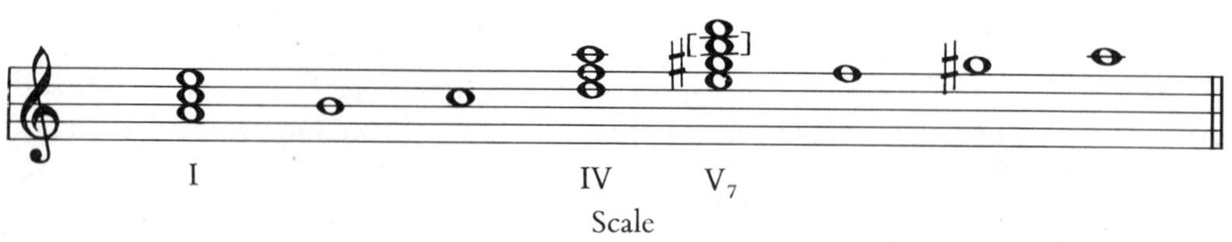

I
IV
V7
Scale

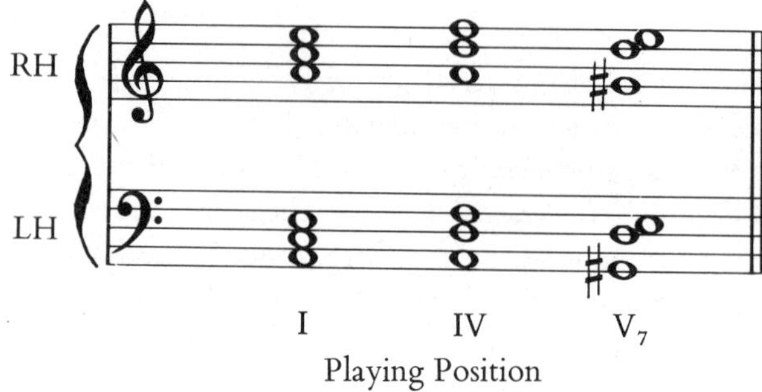

RH
LH
I
IV
V7
Playing Position

Example 3: B♭ Major

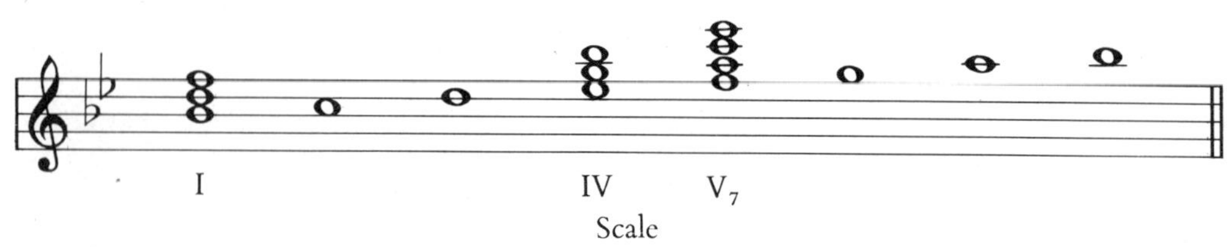

I
IV
V7
Scale

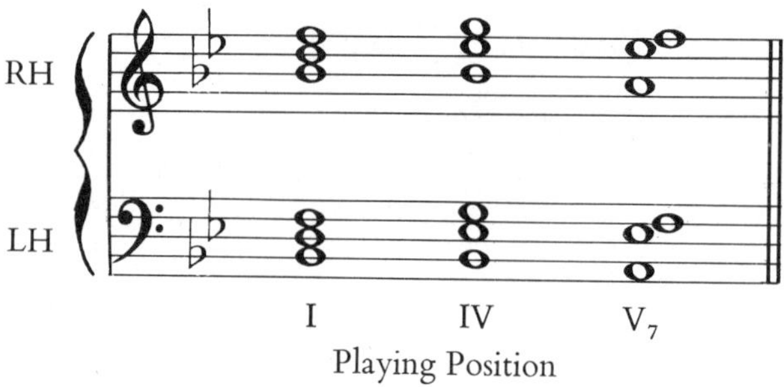

RH
LH
I
IV
V7
Playing Position

Example 4: G Harmonic Minor

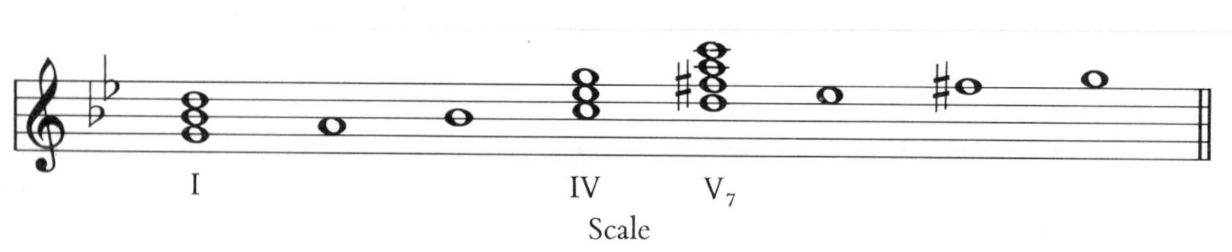

I
IV
V7
Scale

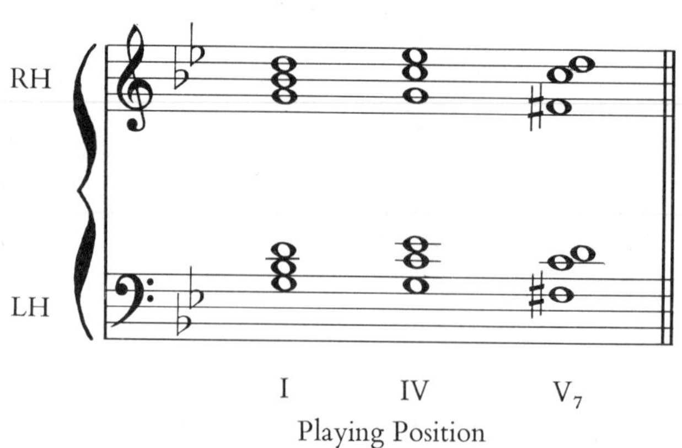

RH
LH
I
IV
V7
Playing Position

Example 5: F Major

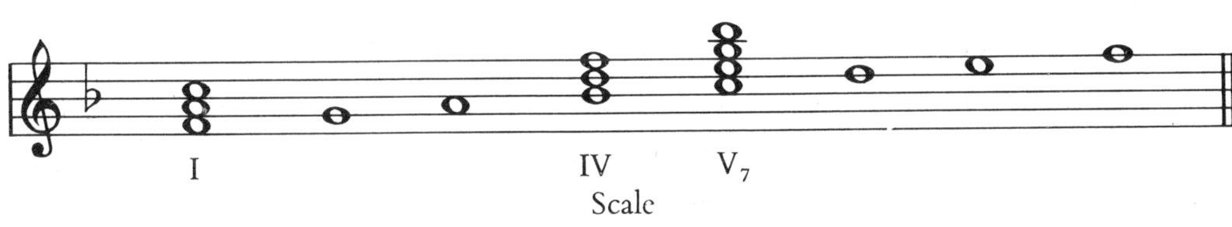
I
IV
V_7
Scale

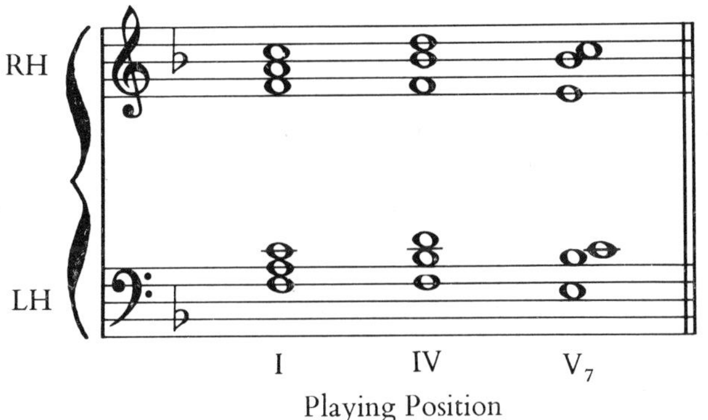
RH
LH
I
IV
V_7
Playing Position

Example 6: D Harmonic Minor

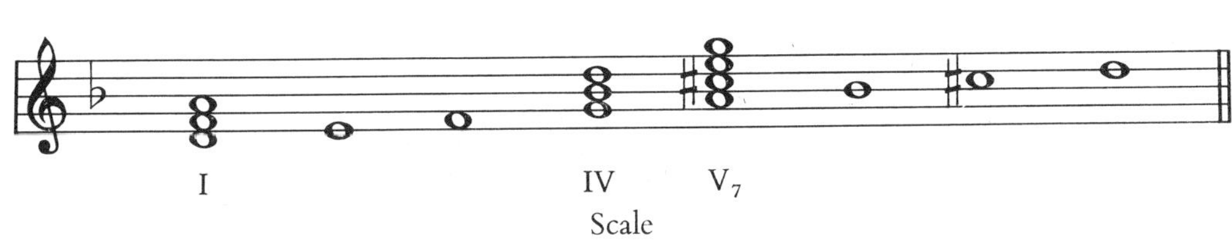
I
IV
V_7
Scale

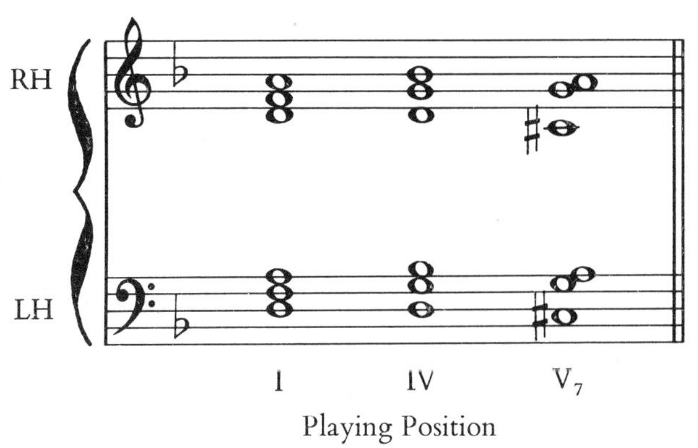
RH
LH
I
IV
V_7
Playing Position

Example 7: G Major

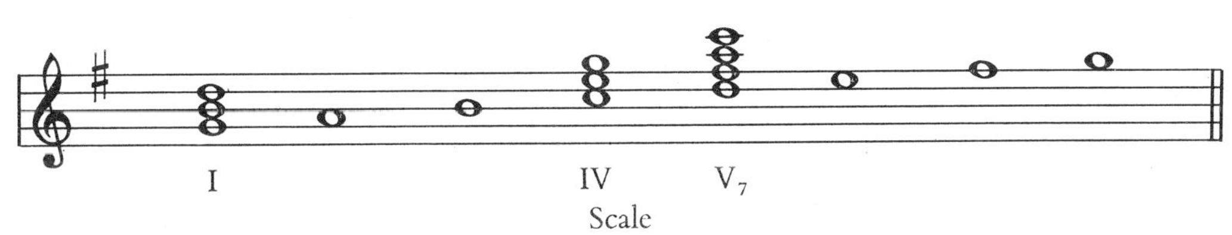
I
IV
V_7
Scale

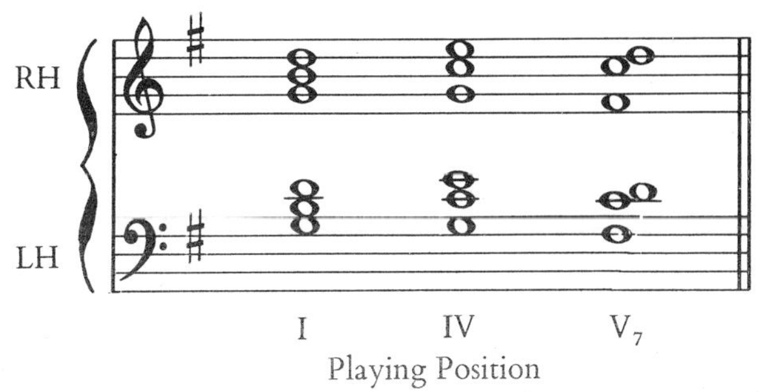
RH
LH
I
IV
V_7
Playing Position

Example 8: E Harmonic Minor

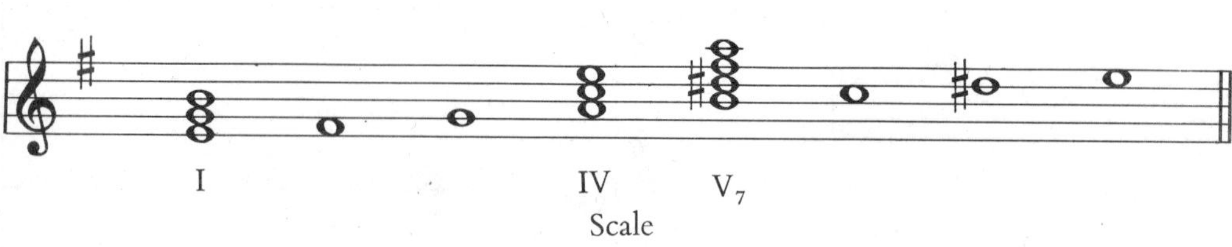

I
IV
V_7
Scale

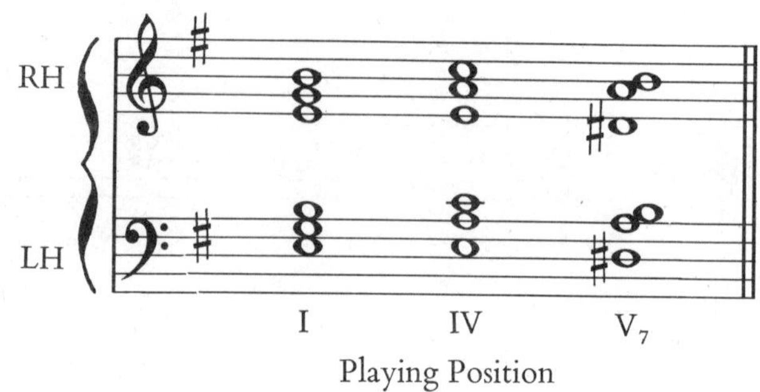

RH
LH
I
IV
V_7
Playing Position

Example 9: D Major

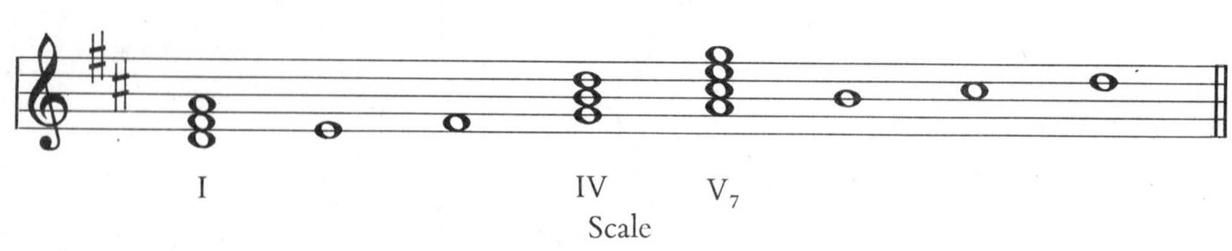

I
IV
V_7
Scale

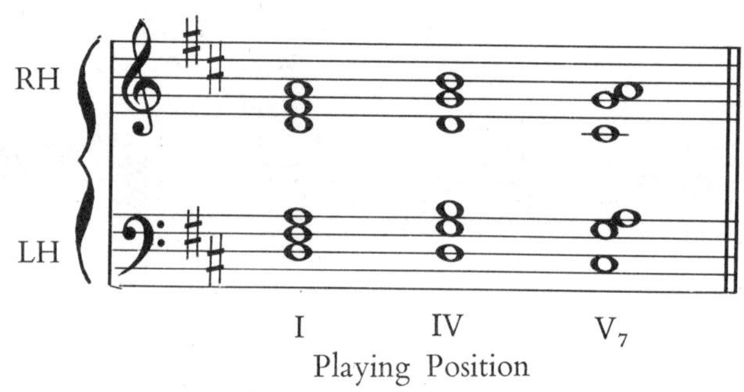

RH
LH
I
IV
V_7
Playing Position

Example 10: B Harmonic Minor

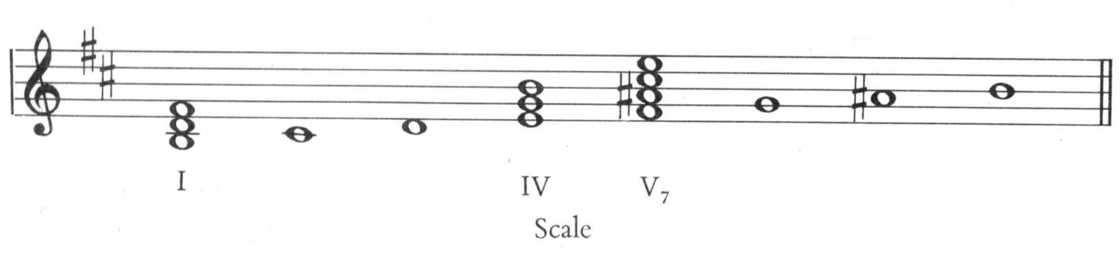

I
IV
V_7
Scale

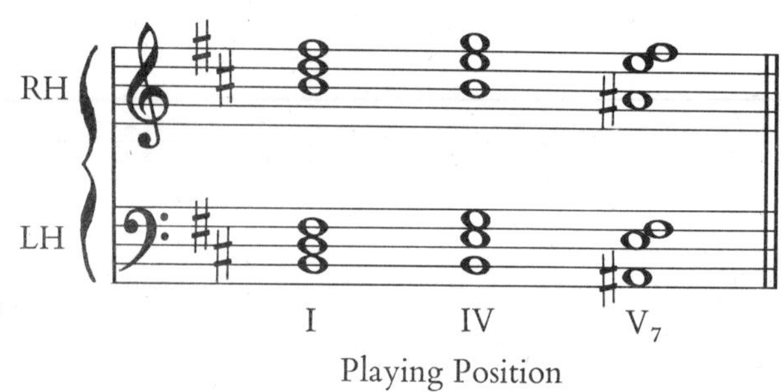

RH
LH
I
IV
V_7
Playing Position

At this point, it is necessary to define one additional harmony—the major SUPERTONIC SEVENTH (II_7). This chord is often referred to as the *Dominant of the Dominant*. It is constructed in the same manner as the V_7—a major triad with an added third placed on top. Supertonic is the name given to the second degree of the scale.

Example 1: C Major

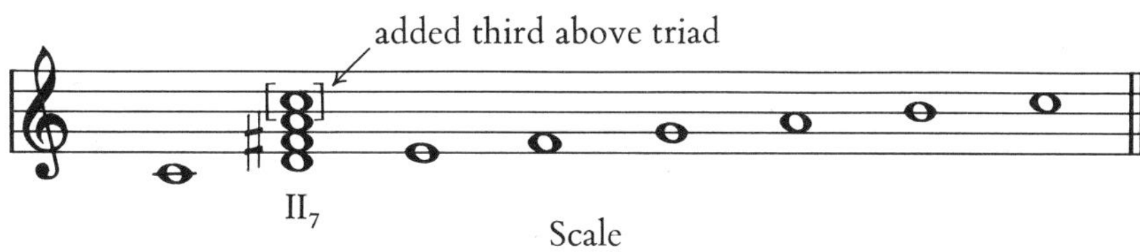
added third above triad
II_7
Scale

In the example above, note that the raised third of the triad (F♯) is necessary to make the triad major. Additional examples follow:

Example 2: G Major

II_7
Scale

Example 3: F Major

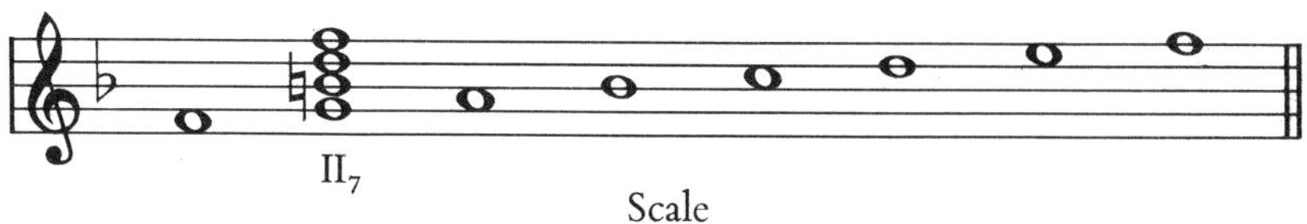
II_7
Scale

To construct this seventh chord in playing position, follow the same procedure as with the V_7, since it essentially has the same function.

Example 4: D Major

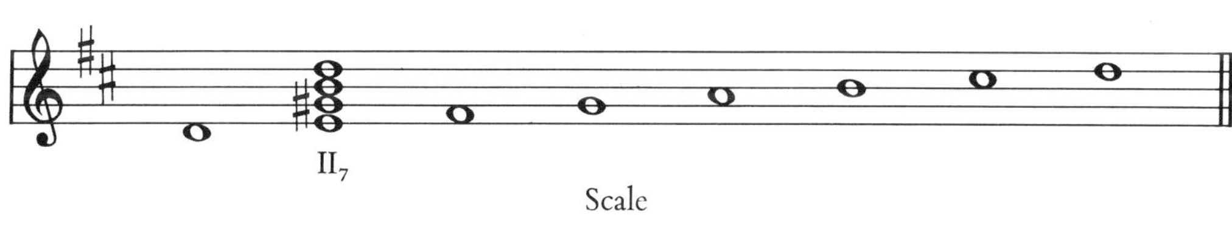
II_7
Scale

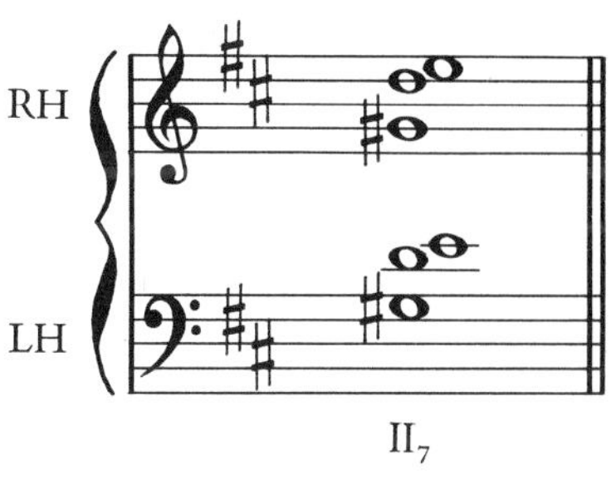
RH
LH
II_7
Playing Position

Following is a song in which the major II_7 has been used:

THE FARMER IN THE DELL

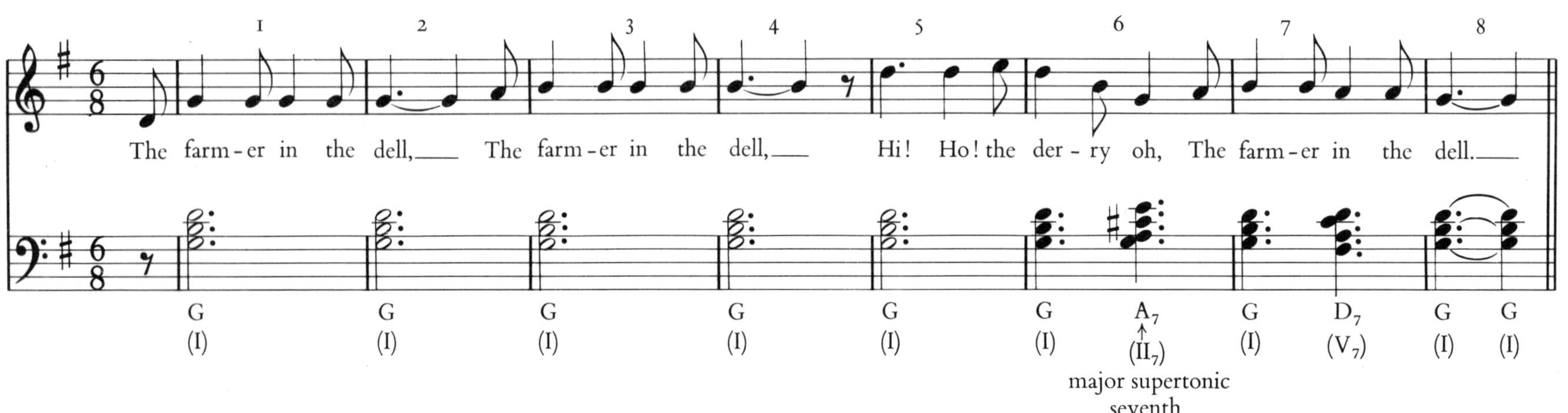

1 2 3 4 5 6 7 8
The farm-er in the dell,___ The farm-er in the dell,___ Hi! Ho! the der-ry oh, The farm-er in the dell.___
G (I) G (I) G (I) G (I) G (I) G (I) A7 (II7) G (I) D7 (V7) G (I) G (I)
major supertonic seventh

2. *Chord Tones*

Notes contained in each of the chords, or harmonies, are called CHORD TONES. For example, the chord tones of the *tonic chord* in the key of F major are F-A-C. The chord tones of the *subdominant chord* in the key of F major are B♭-D-F. The chord tones of the *dominant seventh chord* in the key of F major are C-E-G-B♭.

F Major

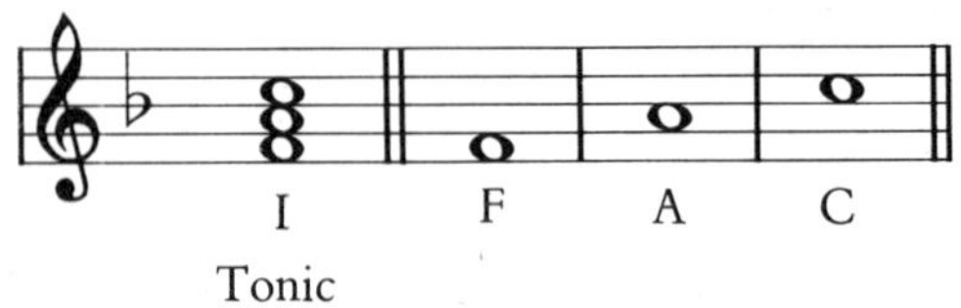

I F A C
Tonic

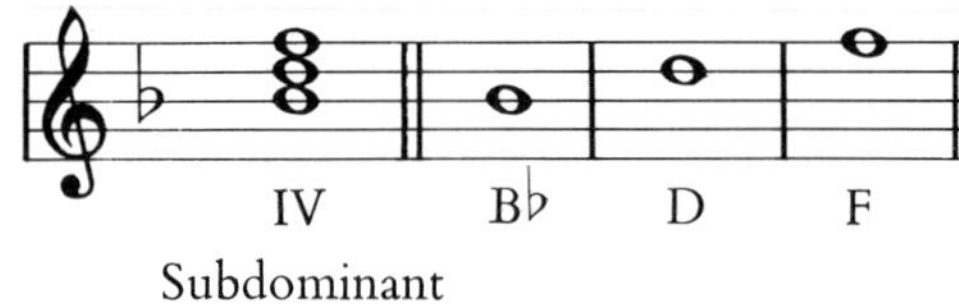

IV B♭ D F
Subdominant

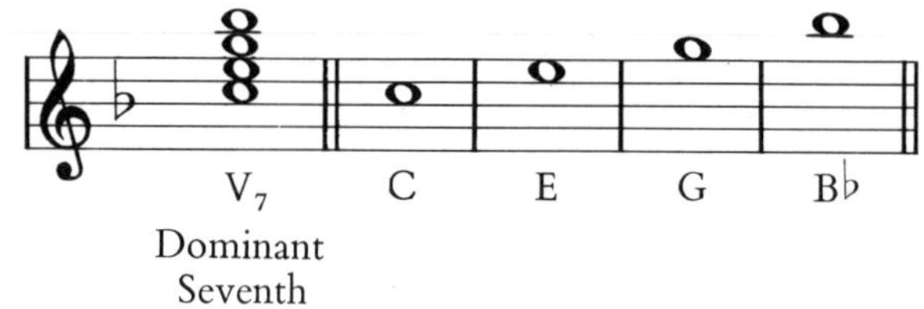

V7 C E G B♭
Dominant Seventh

3. Non-chord Tones

Tones which are in the key, but which are not members of the harmony (chords), are labeled as NON-CHORD TONES.

F Major

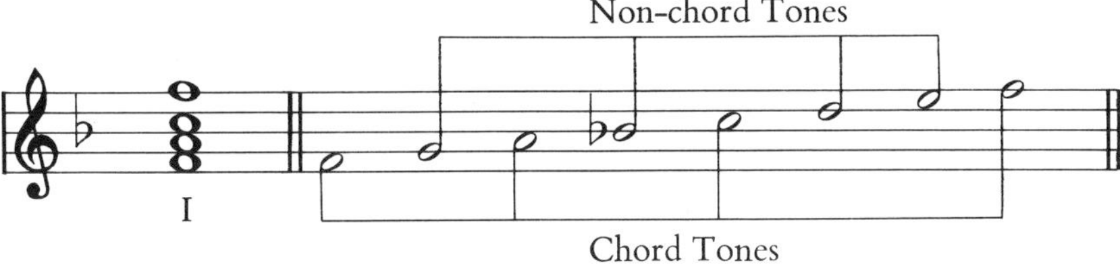
Non-chord Tones
I
Chord Tones

There are several different non-harmonic devices available to the composer. However, for our purpose, and considering the limitations prescribed in this book, only three will be defined—*passing tones*, *upper and lower neighboring tones*, and *appoggiatura*. These devices permit one to add to the singability of a melodic line and enhance its musicality.

A PASSING TONE is a non-chord tone that is found stepwise between chord tones of different pitch.

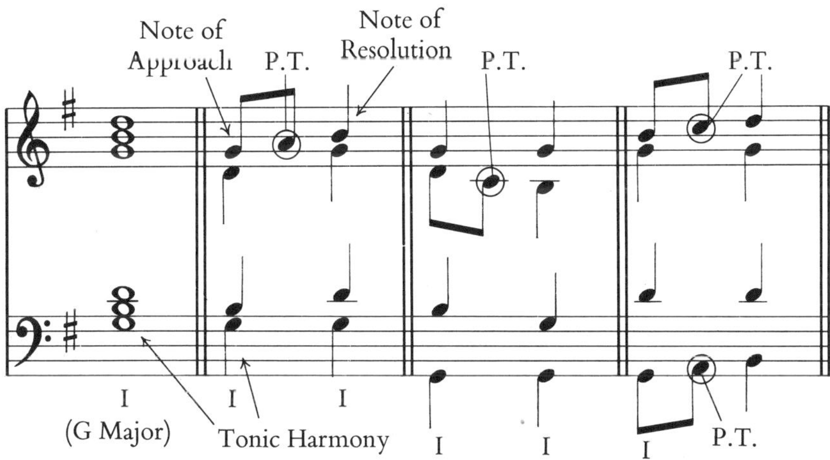
Note of Approach
P.T.
Note of Resolution
P.T.
P.T.
I
(G Major)
I
I
Tonic Harmony
I
I
I
P.T.

Each measure in the above example is supported by tonic harmony.

UPPER AND LOWER NEIGHBORING TONES are non-chord tones that are found stepwise between two chord tones of the *same* pitch.

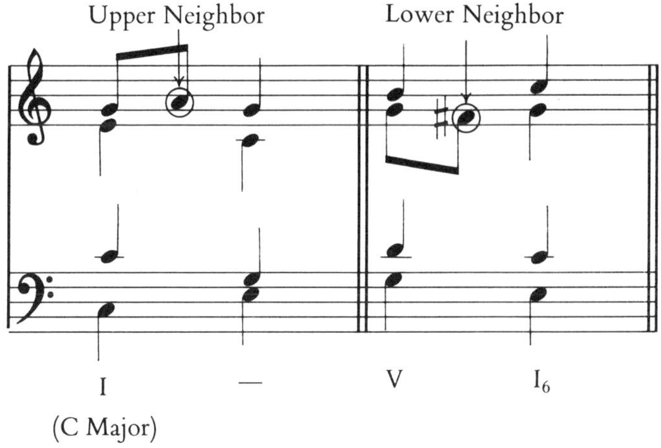
Upper Neighbor
Lower Neighbor
I
—
V
I6
(C Major)

An APPOGGIATURA is a dissonance created by a leap (interval of a third or larger) and resolving stepwise.

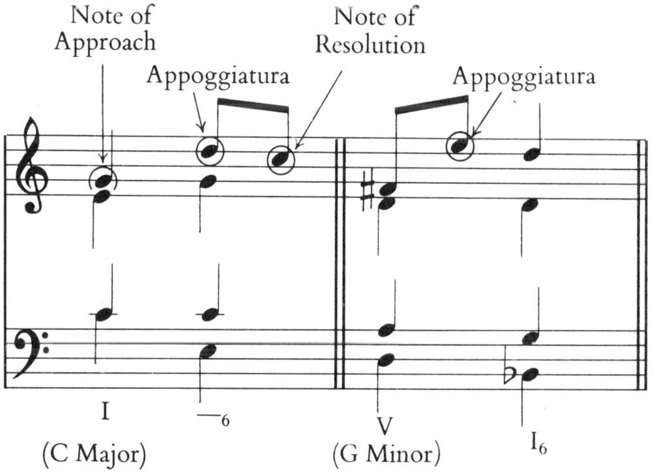
Note of Approach
Appoggiatura
Note of Resolution
Appoggiatura
I
—6
V
I6
(C Major)
(G Minor)

The following melodic fragment is made up entirely of tones found in the tonic chord of F major. Consequently, tonic harmony would satisfactorily support this melodic fragment.

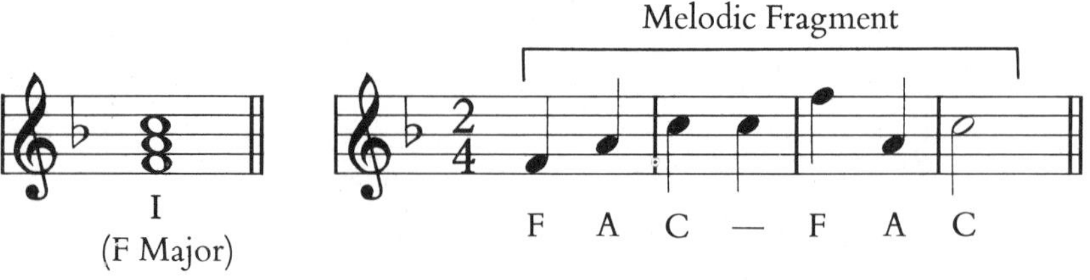
Melodic Fragment
I
(F Major)
F A C — F A C

By cautiously inserting a few *passing tones* (P.T.), the "flow" of the line is improved.

P.T.
P.T.
P.T.

NOTE: It should be pointed out that increasing the *number* of non-chord tones does not necessarily make a melody better! It simply permits the composer greater flexibility.

The above example shows where passing tones could be added, in terms of theoretical possibilities. The student may wish to employ all possible non-chord devices in a certain melody—or only one. This depends entirely on one's taste and the level of proficiency of the performers.

The following example shows the same melodic fragment (without passing tones) with the addition of a *lower neighboring tone*. (L.N. denotes lower neighbor.)

L.N.

The following illustrates how the original chordlike melodic fragment looks with the help of a *passing tone*, a *lower neighboring tone*, and an *appoggiatura*.

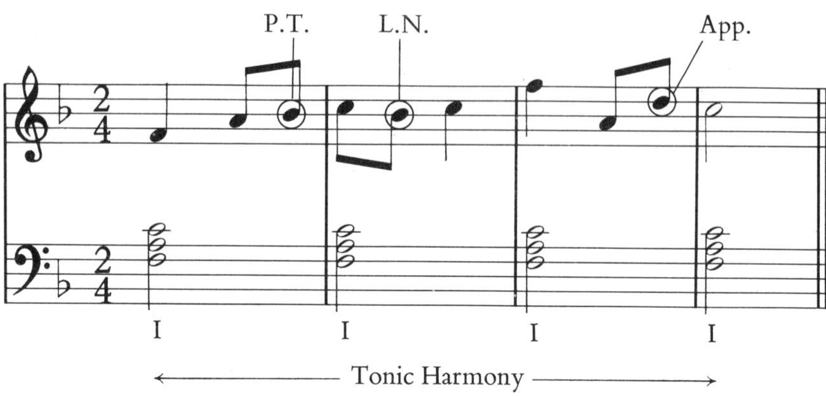
P.T.
L.N.
App.
I
I
I
I
Tonic Harmony

The following fragments of melodies illustrate how the passing tone, upper and lower neighbor, and appoggiatura have been used. Each melodic fragment has a particular, basic harmony.

Example 1: OLD BLUE

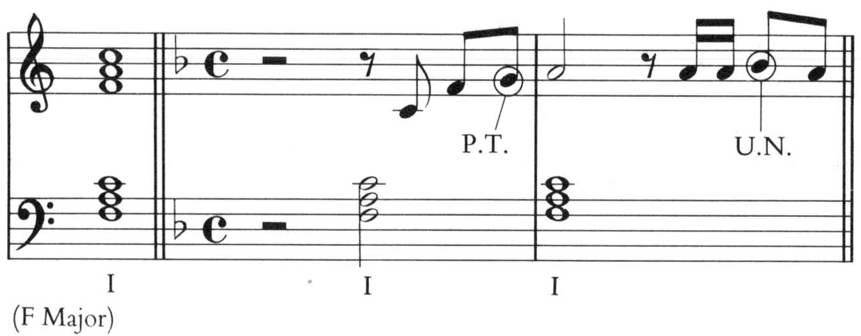
P.T.
U.N.
I
(F Major)
I
I

Example 2: OH WHERE, OH WHERE HAS MY LITTLE DOG GONE

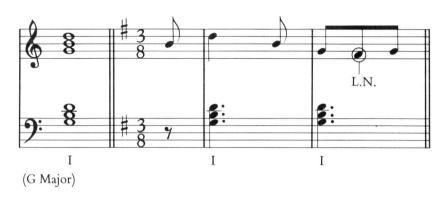

L.N.

I I I

(G Major)

Example 3: SING A SONG OF SIXPENCE

U.N.
I
I
(D Major)

Example 4: YANKEE DOODLE

U.N.
P.T.
P.T.
I
I
I
(B♭ Major)

The student should now do some outside work that will help her become more familiar with non-chord tones. Look through children's music literature to find songs in which these devices have been used. This is the best way to become more familiar with them. It is suggested that all the different types be sought (P.T., U.N. & L.N., and App.).

4. Descant

A DESCANT is an additional melody which is written in *counterpoint* to the original line.

NOTE: It is suggested that when these melodies are written that special consideration be given to the particular *performing medium* that is to be used. For instance, wide intervals, or skips, in the melodic structure are not singable, but could be easily handled by instrumentalists. The flutophone-type of melody instrument is recommended for use in the classroom. The range of children's voices should be kept in mind when structuring descants to be sung. Also, it must be remembered that children should not be forced to sing at a very high or low range.

Following is an example showing the original melody with a descant (or melody 2):

DOWN BY THE STATION

1
2
3
4
5
Descant, or Melody 2
Original Melody
Down by the sta - tion, ear - ly in the morn - ing. See the lit - tle
Primary Harmony
I
I
V7
I
I

6
7
8
9
10
en - gines all in a row, I can see the en - gi - neer,
I
V7
I
I
I

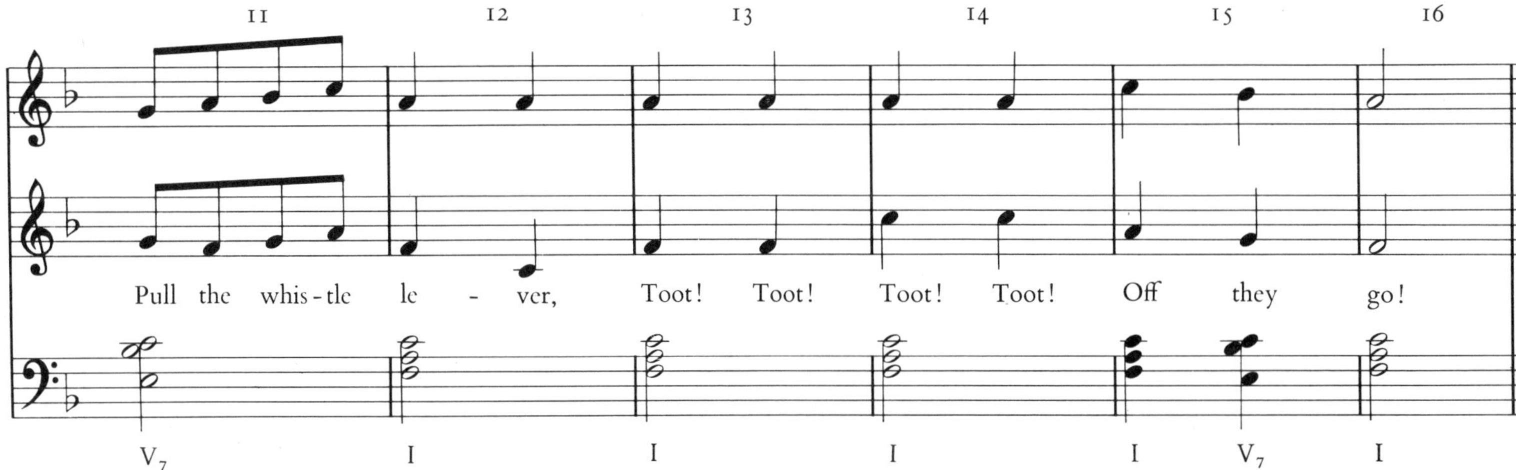
11
12
13
14
15
16
Pull the whis-tle le - ver, Toot! Toot! Toot! Toot! Off they go!
V7
I
I
I
I
V7
I

B. Procedure for Melodic Orchestration

1. Defining Primary Harmonies Within a Given Melody

Many of the elementary school music education books include chord symbols written either above or directly beneath the music notation. These symbols designate by letter names the root tone of the desired chords. For example, if a certain musical selection were to be harmonized by the I, IV, and V_7 chords in the key of F major, the appropriate letter names would be F, B♭, and C_7, respectively. Using the same roman numerals in the key of G major, the letter names would be G, C, and D_7.

In music in which the writers have omitted these harmonic notations, it will be necessary for the student to analyze the melody to determine the chords that should support it. As a general rule, start out by defining only one harmony per measure. Most melodies for children are very satisfactorily harmonized using this delimitation. It must be remembered, however, that this is only a general rule. With repeated practice, students will become increasingly aware of those places in the music where more than one chord per measure is necessary.

The following musical example, "On Top of Old Smoky," is used to illustrate the procedure for *defining the PRIMARY HARMONIES when the printed score does not include them.*

STEP 1: Determine the key and spell out the primary chords. The following example is in the key of C, and the chords are *tonic:* C-E-G; *subdominant:* F-A-C; and *dominant:* G-B-D.

NOTE: Since most dominant chord formations use the added seventh (V_7), subsequent spellings will be structured in this manner. Consequently, this example will use the spelling of dominant harmony as G-B-D-F, the "F" being the added seventh.

STEP 2: Scan the melody to find those places where the melodic line literally "spells out" the different harmonies. Below, these are bracketed and labeled.

Tonic
Tonic

In many pieces, the melody is so chordal in texture that the two steps are all that is necessary.

STEP 3: See if there is consecutive use of chord tones extending beyond the limits of just one measure. The analysis here reveals a repeated use of the tones F-A-C, or *subdominant* harmony.

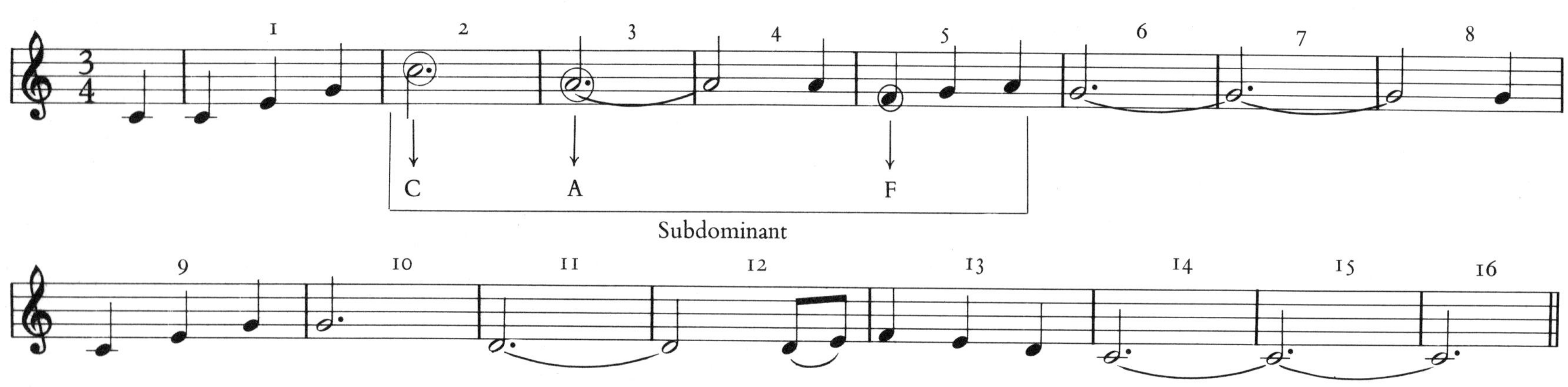
C
A
F
Subdominant

STEP 4: Now that two of the three primary harmonies have been utilized, it leaves us to survey the possibility of using the V_7 harmony. The next analysis shows that three of the four tones in the *dominant* (V_7) chord are used, suggesting a strong possibility that this would prove to be a satisfactory harmonic support for this part of the melody.

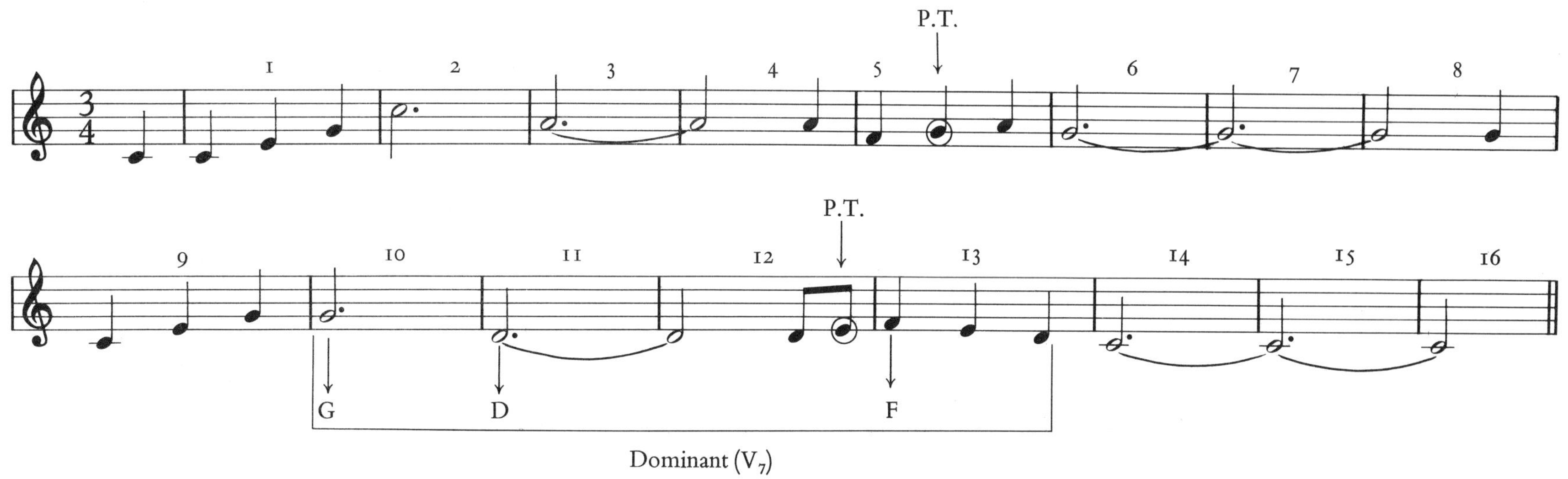
P.T.
1
2
3
4
5
6
7
8
P.T.
9
10
11
12
13
14
15
16
G
D
F
Dominant (V7)

NOTE: It should not be construed that *all* three chords should be used *all* the time in every piece of music. Many melodies are quite adequately harmonized with two, or even one chord.

This leaves measures 6, 7, and 8, and the last three measures without supporting harmony. Here we must be aware of two additional facts:

1. Musical selections that are used in elementary classroom situations *always* end on *tonic* harmony. Thus, the last three measures here would have the chord of the tonic in C major (notes C-E-G) supporting the final tone, "C."
2. Most elementary tunes are structured in easily recognized phrase groupings. A musical phrase is defined as being of either 2 or 4 measure lengths or multiples of such, expressing one musical idea. Notice in measure 8, ending with beat 2, there is an obvious pause, or "breathing point." At these phrase points, the *dominant* harmony is usually the most agreeable in sound.

NOTE: It may be easier for the student to equate musical phrases with prose or narrative, where grammatical phrases are observed by the use of commas, semi-colons, or colons.

Since the note in the melody at this phrase point, measure 6, is G, the use of a V_7 chord is suggested. The complete chordal analysis now appears to be:

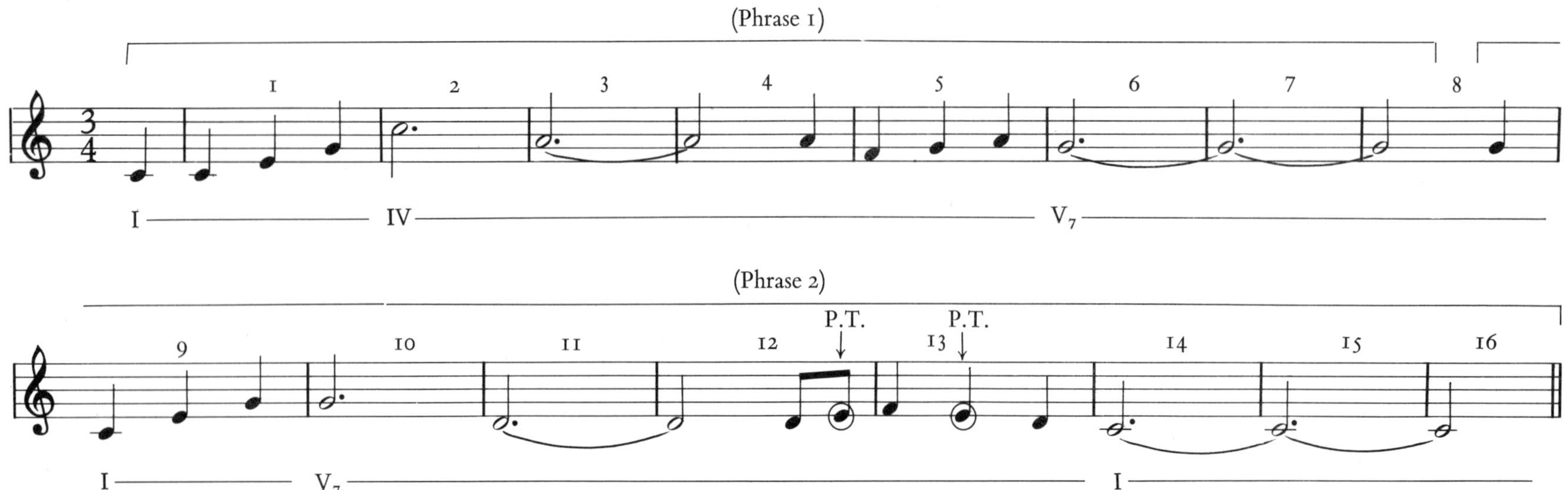

(Phrase 1)
1 2 3 4 5 6 7 8
I IV V7
(Phrase 2)
P.T. P.T.
9 10 11 12 13 14 15 16
I V7 I

STEP 5: Before final determination is made concerning chord structure, the student should "try out" the proposed harmonies at the keyboard. After hearing them, it may be that corrections should be made in some cases. In order to do this a list of chords that contain the note(s) found in the melody should be placed directly beneath the melody. For instance, in measure 2 the student should also consider the tonic chord because it contains a C. In measures 6 and 10 the tonic chord should again be considered because it contains a G. Still other chord possibilities, such as those indicated in parentheses below, can be discovered by this "trial and error" method.

1 2 3 4 5 6 7 8
I IV (I) V7 (I)
9 10 11 12 13 14 15 16
I V7 I (IV)

Taking into consideration all these possibilities for chordal support, the student should now go to the keyboard and try out each combination until the most obviously correct sound is achieved. The following combination of chords is suggested:

P.T.
1 2 3 4 5 6 7 8
I IV I V7 I
P.T. P.T.
9 10 11 12 13 14 15 16
V7 I IV I

The following examples further illustrate the analysis, or definition, of chords within given melodies.

Example 1: RED RIVER VALLEY

P.T. U.N. P.T.
1 2 3 4
I IV I V7 I
P.T. P.T. App. P.T.
5 6 7 8
IV I V7 I

Example 2: DID YOU EVER SEE A LASSIE

U.N. P.T. U.N. P.T.

I — V_7 — I —

— V_7 — I — V_7 — I —

U.N. P.T.

V_7 — I — V_7 — I

Example 3: PAPER OF PINS

L.N.
I
V7
IV
I
V7
I

2. *Evolvement of Descant(s)*

STEP 1: Once the primary harmonies have been derived (see pp. 113–118), they should be notated on the staff above the melody. The notation of the chords usually starts on the first *full* measure. Rhythmic notation is used so that the chord will consume the duration of the entire measure. (In the following melody, "On Top of Old Smoky," the time signature is $\frac{3}{4}$, and the chords are notated as dotted half notes in order to consume the same time as three quarter notes.) The following chord positions (playing positions) are suggested because later on these same patterns will be used in the study of harmonic accompaniment:

I
C
IV
F
I
C
V7
G7
I
C
V7
G7
I
C
IV
F
I
C

The letters that have been placed beneath the symbols for tonic, subdominant, and dominant seventh designate the *root* tones of each of those particular chords.

STEP 2: The "x" placed beside tones on the chord staff in the melody above indicate the initial tones which have been *arbitrarily* chosen to form the "skeleton" of the new melody, or descant. In the selection of the new tones, the student should attempt to:

1. Choose tones that are not repeatedly reproduced in the melody.
2. Avoid consecutive skips of excessively wide intervals.
3. Avoid (as much as possible) repetition of consecutive tones across bar lines.
4. Try to achieve a smooth flowing line.

A descant should be a melody within itself and should be able to stand alone. Contrasting movement between the descant(s) and the original melody should be sought. In evolving descants, it is best to avoid intervals of fourths and fifths at cadence points, that is, places where there are definite pauses. Intervals of thirds, sixths, unisons, and octaves are preferable. In cases similar to the one found in measure 1 of the following selection, the procedure should, generally speaking, be to choose a tone *other* than the one which begins the measure. For example, C is the first tone, so either E or G could be used as the starting tone. *These criteria are listed to help the student get started. Under no circumstances is it suggested that they should be adhered to rigidly. Constant modification and refinement in the creative exercise will insure much improved melodic lines.*

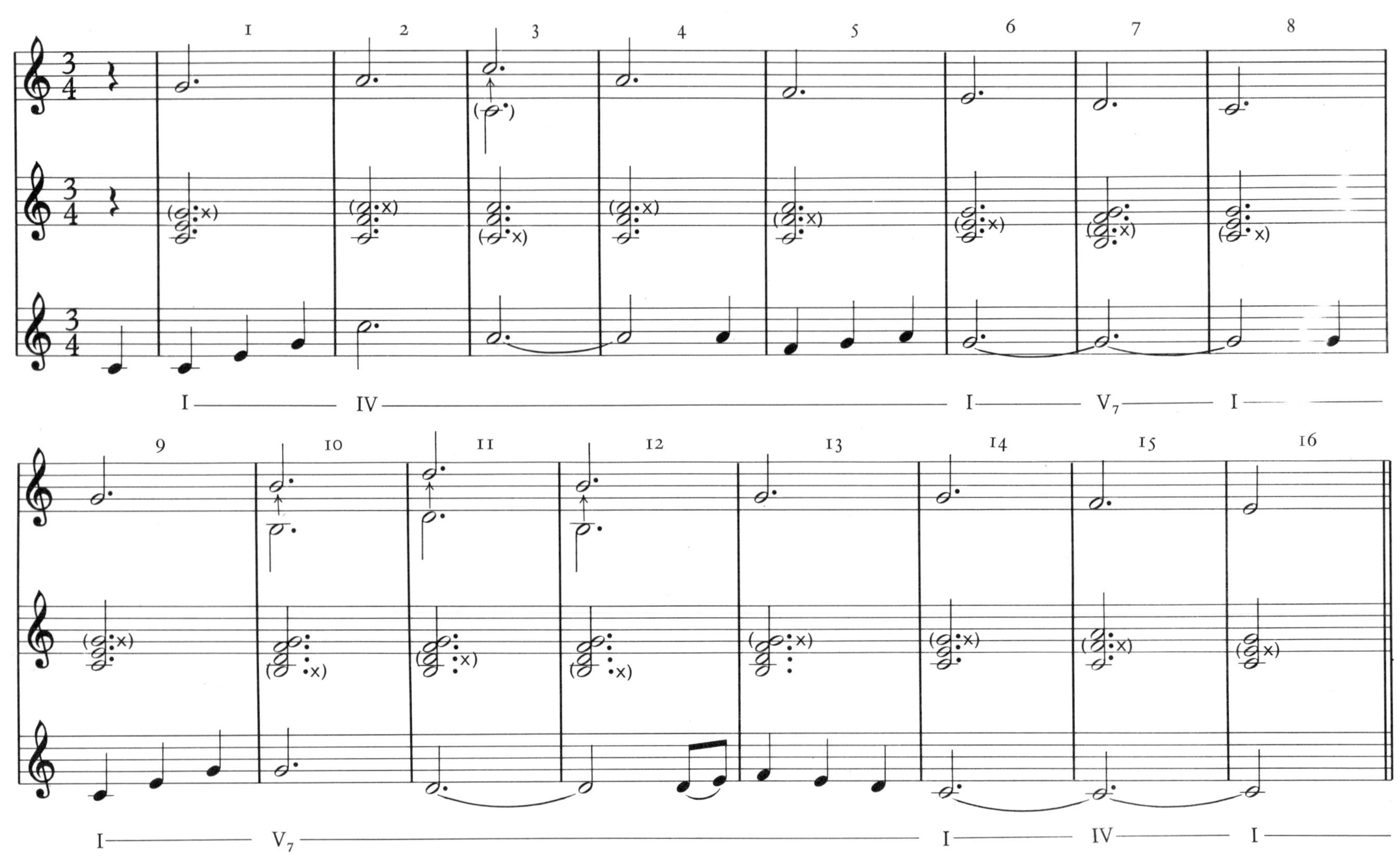

1
2
3
4
5
6
7
8
I
IV
I
V7
I
9
10
11
12
13
14
15
16
I
V7
I
IV
I

NOTE: In measures 3, 10, 11, and 12 the tone has been used in a different position than it occupies in the chord. The tone in parentheses shows the position it had in the chord. The replacing of four of the tones upward an octave (measures 3, 10, 11, 12) was done to realize a smooth flow in the melodic framework.

Thus far, this basic framework (or skeleton) of a new melody has been achieved without the addition of any non-chord tones to the primary harmonies. *Before proceeding further, the student should select other* chord tones *to form still another framework. Constant juggling, or re-positioning, of these available tones will aid greatly in the final selection.*

STEP 3: The next suggested step in the descant evolvement is to determine where added *non-chord* tones would be beneficial. Here, the student has to explore the various possibilities until the sound she is seeking finally takes shape.

NOTE: The student is reminded, however, that overuse of non-chord tones tends to destroy tonality, which is contrary to the tenets of good musical composition.

Observe the use of passing tones in measures 2, 4, 10, and 12.

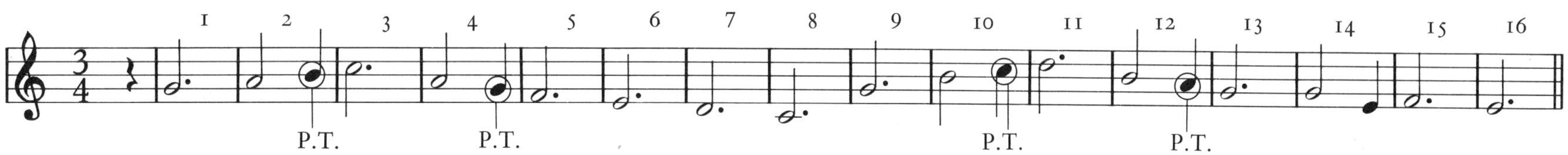

1 2 3 4 5 6 7 8 9 10 11 12 13 14 15 16
P.T.
P.T.
P.T.
P.T.

These non-chord tone insertions help break the monotony of the dotted half note rhythmic structure.

Obviously, more passing tones *could* be used in this new melody. But before these are added, the student might well consider the performing proficiency level of the pupils for whom the melody is to be written. A rhythmic adjustment must be made if the teacher intends to use the same text that is written. In this case, compatibility can be achieved by simply repeating whatever notes are necessary to flow rhythmically with the text. If, however, this line is to be performed by melody instruments, individuality should be sought in the rhythmic and melodic structures.

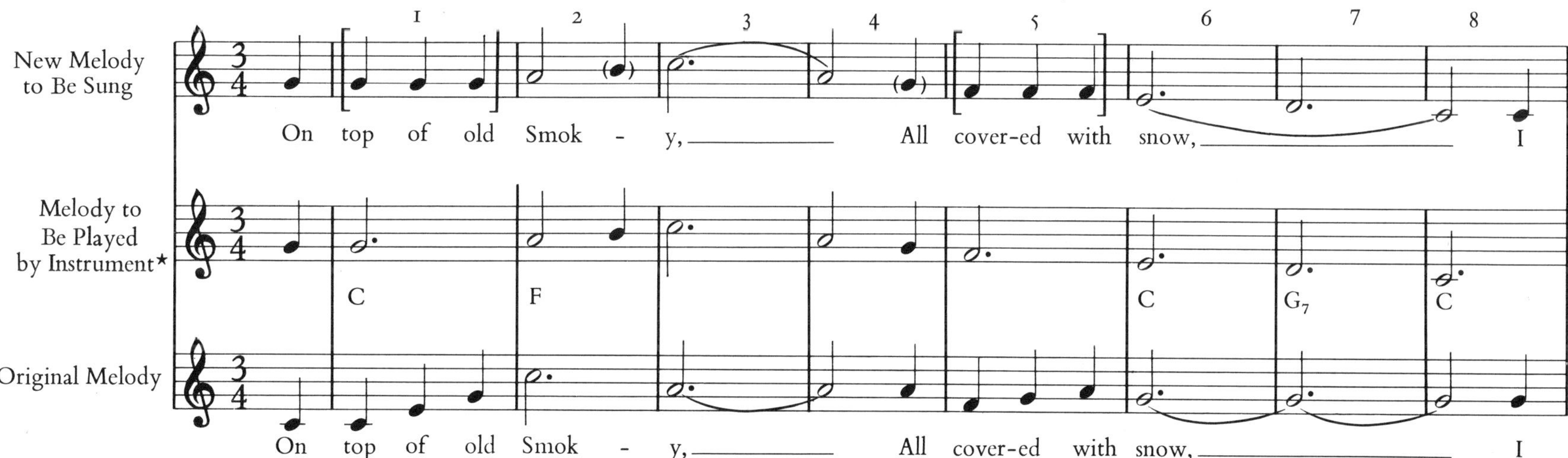

New Melody to Be Sung
1 2 3 4 5 6 7 8
On top of old Smok - y, All cover-ed with snow, I
Melody to Be Played by Instrument*
C F C G7 C
Original Melody
On top of old Smok - y, All cover-ed with snow, I

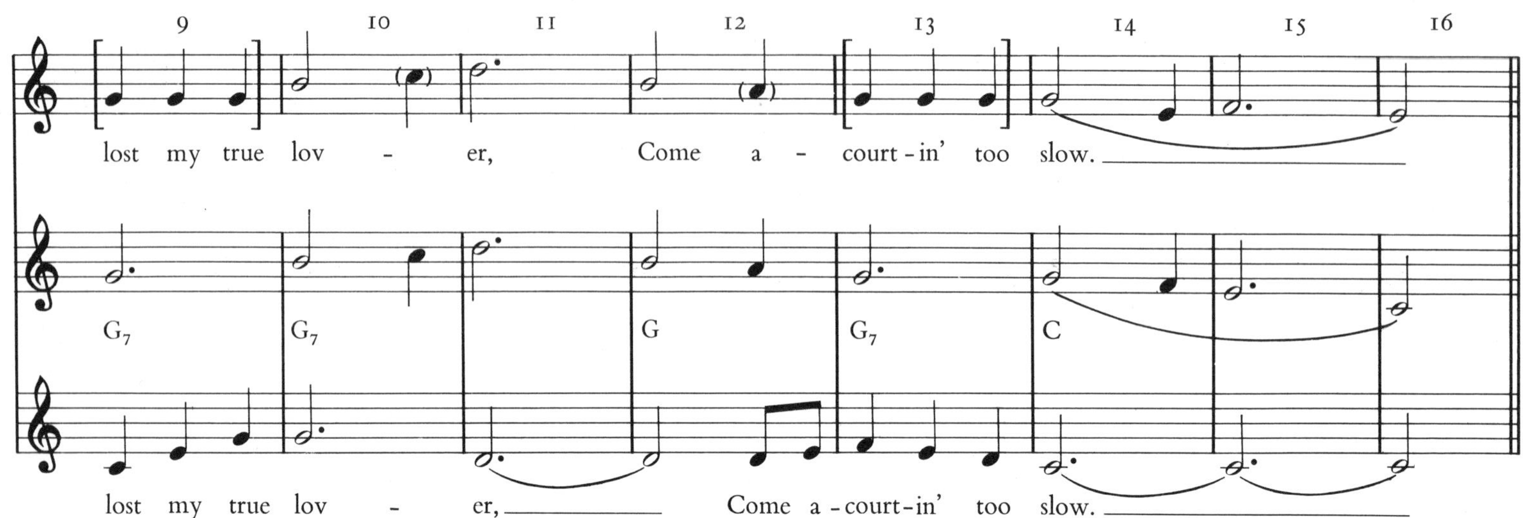
9
10
11
12
13
14
15
16
lost my true lov - er, Come a - court - in' too slow.
G7 G7 G G7 C
lost my true lov - er, Come a - court - in' too slow.

[ ] Repeated notes to make vocal descant compatible with text. ★ In preparing the instrumental melody, the student should take into account the range of the instrument. For instance, if flutophones are used, the range is from [staff]. The above melody lies within the range of this instrument.

Since the four instances of repeated tones (bracketed notes) do create some monotony, it would be well to consider some kind of alteration. In the first bracket the second G might go down to E, a chord-tone, to give a little contrary motion to the given melody line:

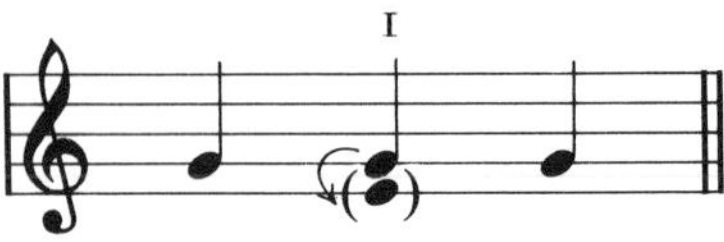
1

In the second group of bracketed notes, we could use the same idea and go in the opposite direction to chord-tone A:

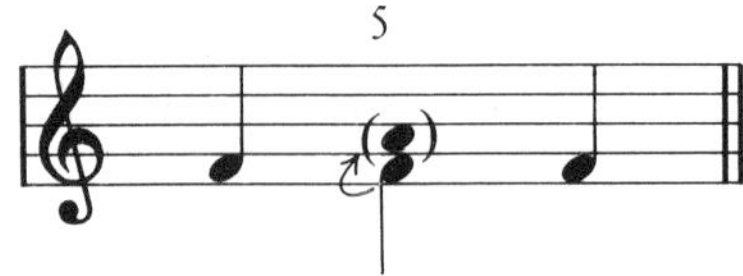
5

The third group is the beginning of the second phrase, thus suggesting the use of the same pattern as in the first group (measure 9). In the fourth group (measure 13), a B is suggested, providing opposite movement to the ultimate direction and conclusion of the melody:

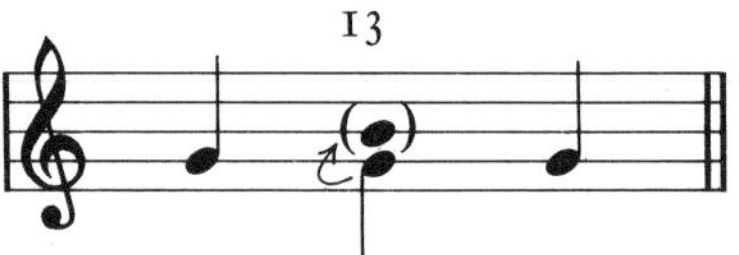
13

With these additions, plus the insertion of non-chord tones, the melody could easily be performed by singing groups as well as instrumental groups. *In fact, it is felt that* mixing *singing with the playing of instruments would be highly beneficial to the children.*

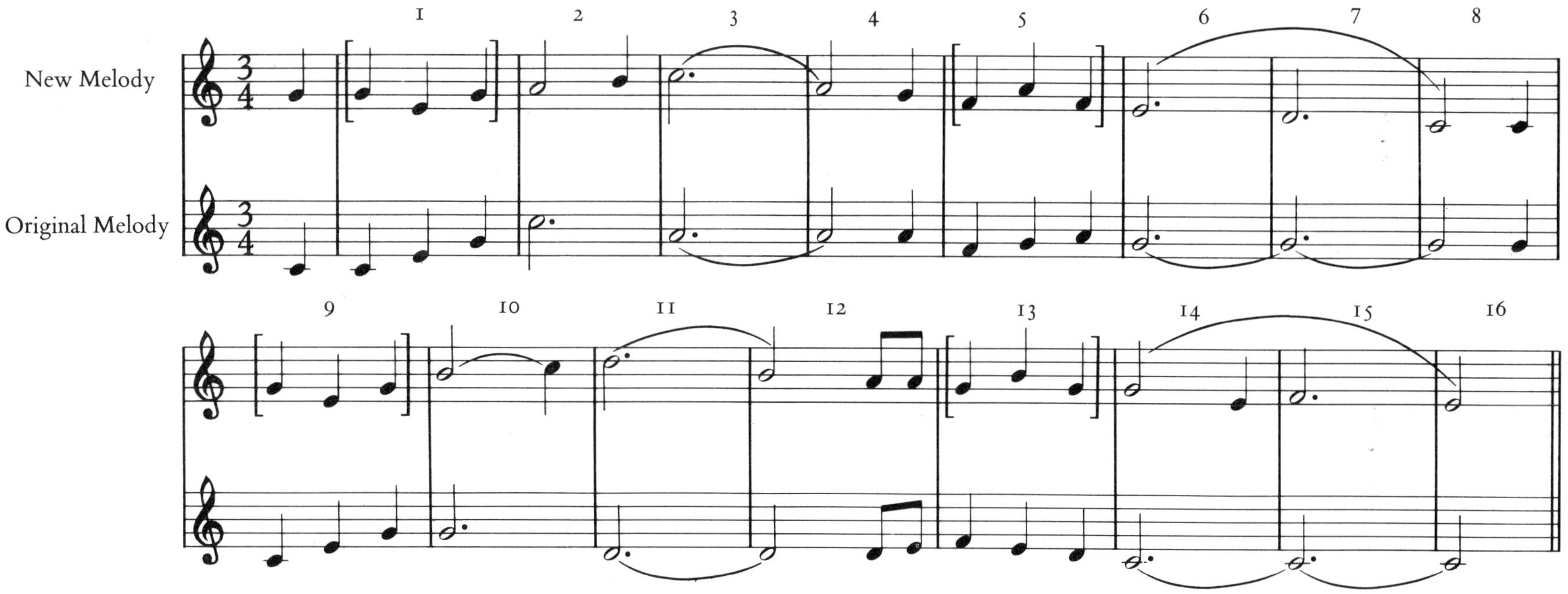
New Melody
Original Melody
1
2
3
4
5
6
7
8
9
10
11
12
13
14
15
16

Summary of Descant Evolvement

5
On top of old Smok - - y,
All cov - ered with snow,
P.T.
P.T.
4
3
2
C
F
F
F
F
C
G_7
1
On top of old Smok - - y,
All cov - ered with snow,

I lost my true lov - - er, Come a - court - in' too slow.
P.T.
P.T.
C
C
G7
G7
G7
G7
C
F
C
I lost my true lov - - er, Come a - court - in' too slow.

2 Application

The following sets of examples are divided into four groups:

A. *Group 1:* These five-stave selections illustrate further the evolvement process of working from an existing melody to a final descant.

B. *Group 2:* These examples show the final descant scored with the original melody and primary harmonies. These harmonies are notated in the bass clef in "playing position" for performance at the keyboard. *Only chord tones are used in these descants.*

C. *Group 3:* Shown here are examples of descants scored with the original melody and primary harmonies. These melodic structures accommodate vocal and/or instrumental combinations. *Both chord and non-chord tones are used in these descants.*

D. *Group 4:* These are supplementary examples of descant orchestrations.

A. Group 1

EVENING BELLS
England
(Vocal)
P.T.
U.N.
P.T.
U.N.
5
Those eve - ning bells, those eve - ning bells, How many a tale their mu - sic tells, Of
4
3
2
G7
C
G7
C
1
Those eve - ning bells, those eve - ning bells, How many a tale their mu - sic tells, Of

P.T.
App.
P.T.
youth and home and that sweet time, When last I heard their sooth - ing chimes.
G7
C
F
C
F
G7
C
youth and home and that sweet time, When last I heard their sooth - ing chimes.

HOT CROSS BUNS

(Instrumental)
App.
P.T.
P.T.
P.T.
P.T.
England
G
D7
G
D7
G
D7
G
D7
G
Hot cross buns! Hot cross buns! One a pen-ny, two a pen-ny, Hot cross buns!

JUNE NIGHT

(Vocal and/or Instrumental)
Offenbach
VOICES
5
Beau - teous night, O night of love, Smile on our en - chant - ment.
4
3
2
C
G_7
C
I
Beau - teous night, O night of love, Smile thou on our en - chant - ment.

Ra - diant night with stars a - bove Beau - teous night of love.
G7
C
Ra - diant night with stars a - bove, O beau - teous night of love.

B. Group 2

ALOHA OE
Queen Liliuokaloni
Descant*
La, La, La, La,
Original Melody
PIANO
Dear the thoughts I take a-way with me, Sweet mem-'ries of our hap-py past, It is
Primary Harmony
F Bb F C7 —
La, La, La, La.
sad that we must say "Fare-well," In our dreams we shall meet a-gain at last.
F Bb F Bb C7 F

* Since the rhythmic structure of this descant would prohibit vocal performance of the text beneath the original melody, it is suggested that a melody instrument, such as the flutophone, be used; however, vocal renditions can be achieved by producing neutral syllables such as "la," "loo," etc.

THE FARMER IN THE DELL

England

Descant*
Original Melody
PIANO
Primary Harmony
1
2
3
4
The farm - er in the dell, The farm - er in the dell,
The farm - er in the dell, The farm - er in the dell,
5
6
7
8
Hi! Ho! the der - ry oh, The farm - er in the dell.
Hi! Ho! the der - ry oh, The farm - er in the dell.

* The rhythmic notation of this descant has been structured to permit vocal performance, since the rhythms of the descant and the original text are compatible.

GOOD MORNING TO YOU

Anonymous
Descant*
Good morn - ing to you. We're read - y to start a new day.
Original Melody
PIANO
Good morn-ing to you, Good morn-ing to you. We're all in our plac - es, With sun - shin - ing fac - es. Is not this the way, To start a new day?
Primary Harmony

* Observe that this text has been "modified" to permit vocal as well as instrumental performance. Students are encouraged to consider combining singing with instrumental activity.

C. Group 3

HOME

German Folk Tune
Descant*
Original Melody
PIANO
Primary Harmony
Home, home, can I for - get thee? Dear, dear, dear - ly loved home.
F
C7
F

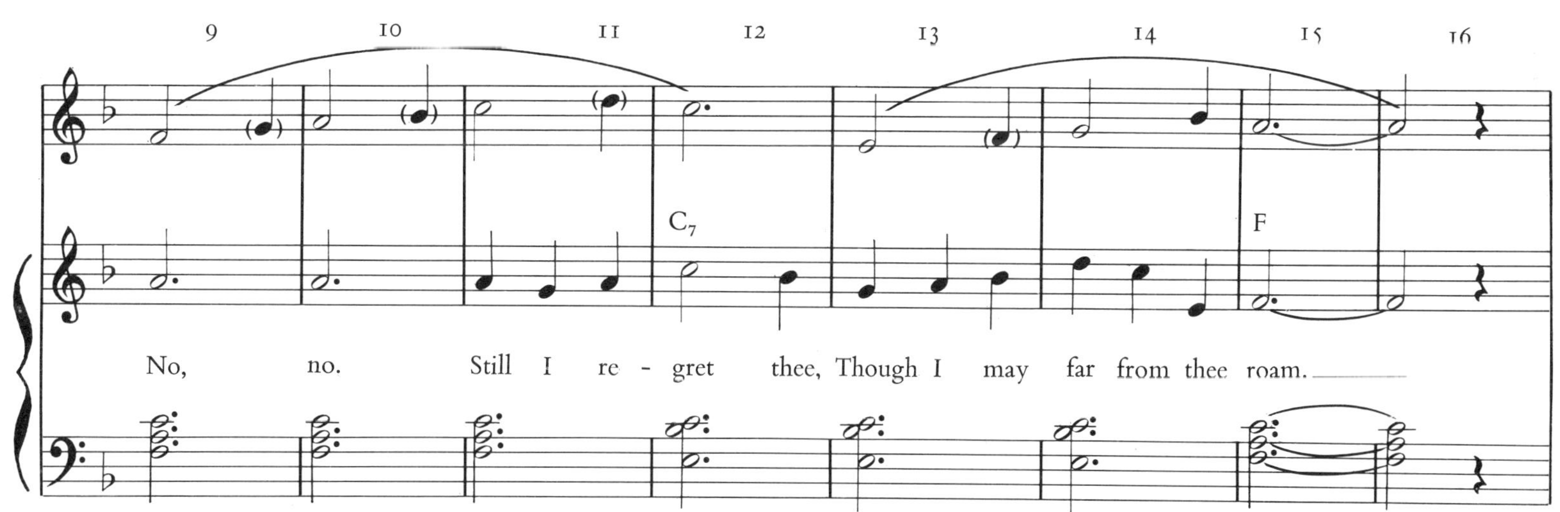
C7
F
No, no. Still I re - gret thee, Though I may far from thee roam.

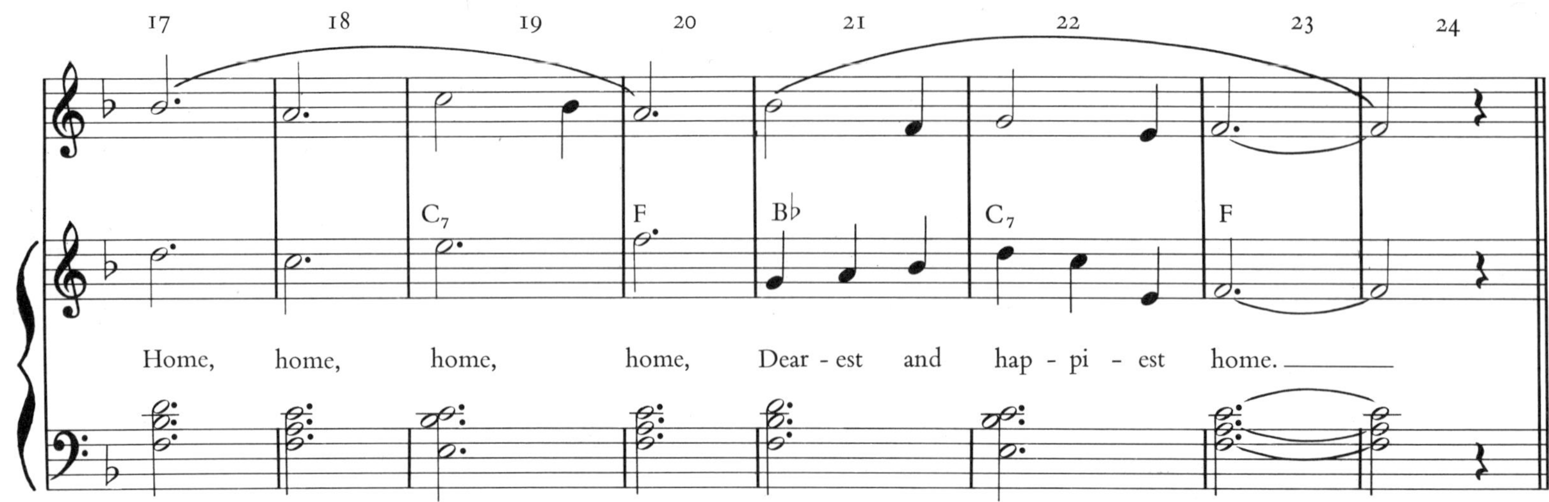
17
18
19
20
21
22
23
24
C7
F
B♭
C7
F
Home, home, home, home, Dear - est and hap - pi - est home.

* Non-chord tones are given in parentheses. The use of passing tones and appoggiatura in this descant provides a more singable line, reducing the intervalic relationship to step-wise, rather than triadic, movement.

MUSIC ALONE SHALL LIVE

Germany

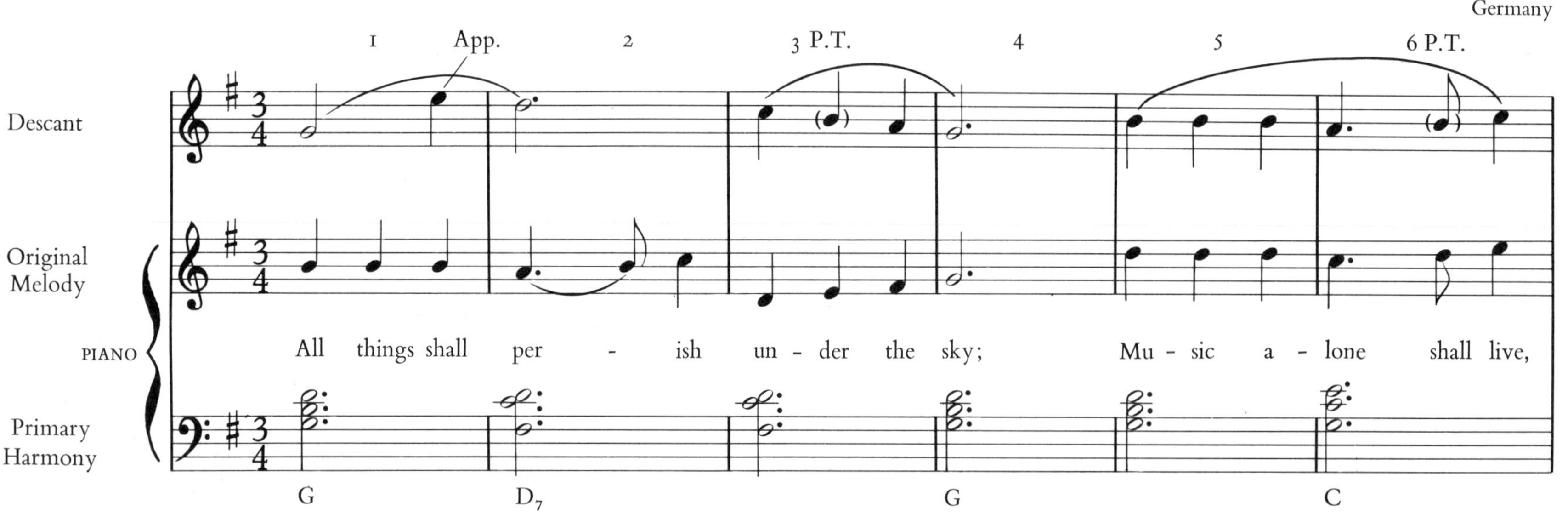
1
App.
2
3 P.T.
4
5
6 P.T.
Descant
Original
Melody
PIANO
Primary
Harmony
All things shall per - ish un - der the sky; Mu - sic a - lone shall live,
G
D7
G
C

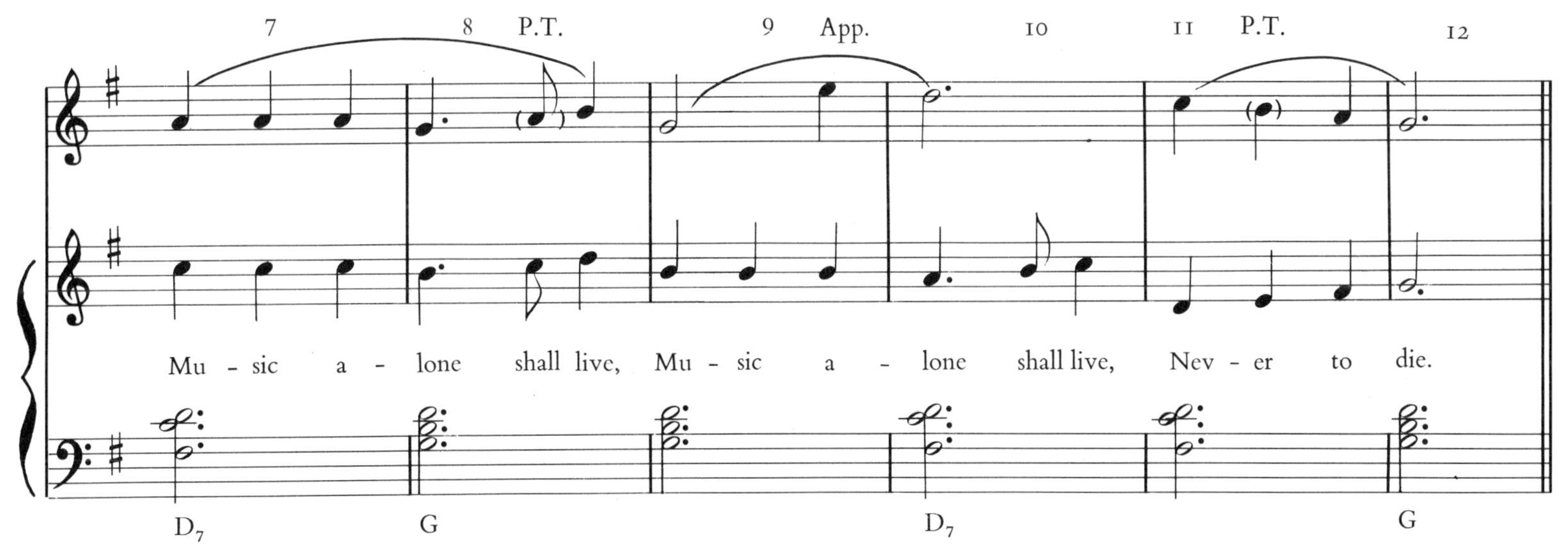
7
8 P.T.
9 App.
10
11 P.T.
12
Mu - sic a - lone shall live, Mu - sic a - lone shall live, Nev - er to die.
D7
G
D7
G

HE'S GOT THE WHOLE WORLD IN HIS HANDS

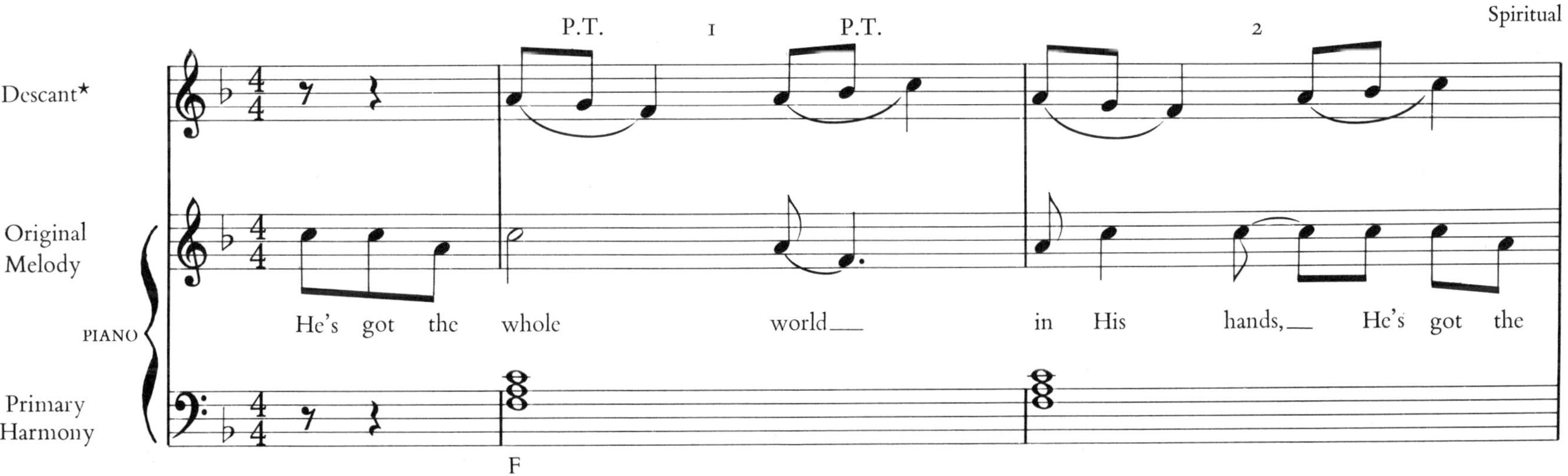
Spiritual
P.T.
1
P.T.
2
Descant*
Original
Melody
PIANO
Primary
Harmony
He's got the whole world__ in His hands,__ He's got the
F

P.T.
3
P.T.
4
5
whole world__ in His hands,__ He's got the whole world__
C7
F
6
7
8
in His hands,__ He's got the whole world in His hands.
C7
F

* This type of musical figure, or motive, could be played very well by a melody instrument such as tone bells.

D. Group 4

CLAP HANDS WITH ME

Italian Melody

Descant (FLUTOPHONES, BELLS)

Original Melody

Come clap hands with me; Come clap hands with me;

Primary Harmony

Join in the game, For it's al - ways the same, Come clap hands with me.

TAP YOUR FEET

Tune adapted from "Old Joe Clark"

Descant (VOICES)
Original Melody
Primary Harmony
Tap, tap, tap, tap, La la la, Tap, tap, tap, tap,
Tap, tap, tap your feet, Tap your feet to - geth - er, Tap, tap,
La la la, La la la,
tap your feet, Tap your feet to - geth - er La la la la la la la,

La la la, La la la, La la la
La la la la la, La la la la la la la, La la la la la

WHOOPEE TI YI YO

United States

Descant 1 (CHIMES, BELLS)

Descant 2 (VOICES)

Oo, — la la, Oo, — la la, Oo, — la la, Oo, —

Original Melody

As I was a - walk - ing one morn - ing for plea - sure, I spied a cow pun - cher a -

Primary Harmony

la la, Oo, la la, Oo, la la, Oo, la
rid - ing a - long. His hat was throwed back, and his spurs were a - jing - ling, And as he ap -
la, Oo, la la. Yi - pi yi! Yi - pi yi! Yi - pi yi! Yi
proached he was sing - ing this song: Whoo-pee ti yi yo, git a - long lit - tle

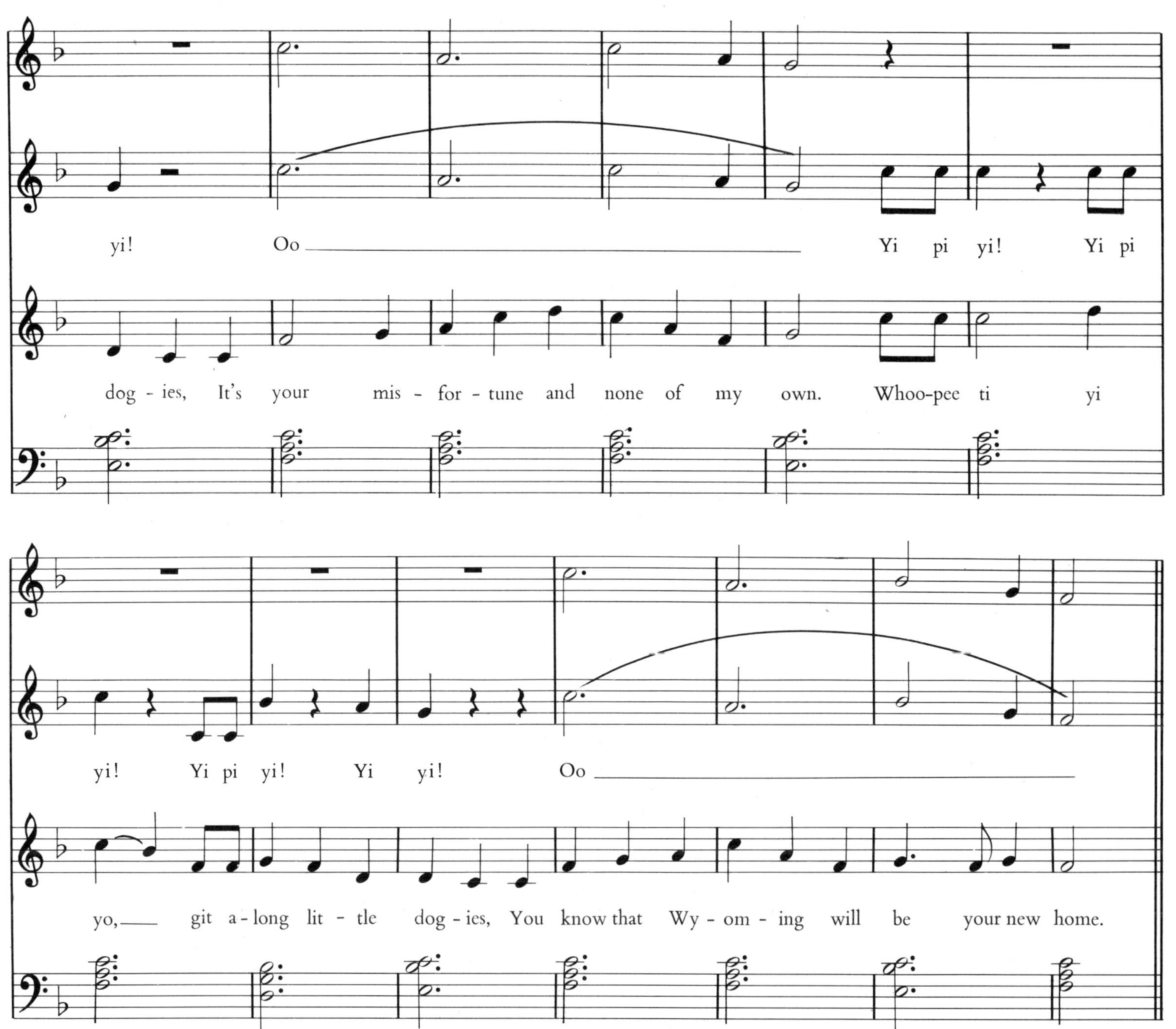
yi! Oo Yi pi yi! Yi pi
dog - ies, It's your mis - for - tune and none of my own. Whoo-pee ti yi
yi! Yi pi yi! Yi yi! Oo
yo, git a - long lit - tle dog - ies, You know that Wy - om - ing will be your new home.

3 Assignments: Student Worksheets

The student worksheets have been divided into three groups:

A. *Group 1:* These worksheets should show evolvement of descants from original melody (staff 1) to final descant (staff 5). The following procedure is suggested for including material on the numbered staves of these worksheets:

Staff 5: Final descant evolvement. (Here, the rhythm should be compatible with text, unless neutral syllables are the desired vocal activity or unless instrumental activity is sought.)

Staff 4: Modification of this outline with additional chord tones, perhaps with the appearance of a few non-chord devices.

Staff 3: Reproduction of a skeleton outline of descant.

Staff 2: Realization of primary harmonies.

Staff 1: Original melody.

B. *Group 2:* A single descant in its *final* form. This score eliminates the previous five-stave score; the student will still evolve the descants in the manner indicated for Group 1, but she will use this score for performance. This melodic line may be constructed for vocal and/or instrumental activity.

C. *Group 3:* Two descants in *final* form. The student should construct these two-part melodic lines for vocal and/or instrumental combinations.

NOTE: The student should review the general criteria for evolving, or creating, melodic descants as found in the section on Evolvement of Descant(s), pp. 129–136. It is further suggested that an open mind be kept with regard to musical creativity. Many, many attempts will need to be made before final determination of a "good melody" is achieved. It is through this constant and consistent effort that lasting benefits will accrue both for the college student and those whom she will teach in future years.

The blank manuscript paper at the end of each group is included for the student to do additional melodic orchestrations. The selection of the music material to be used is left to the discretion of the instructor and/or student. The perforated sheets are included for the purpose of providing individual parts to members of the class performing assigned selections. Need for additional parts will require the student to construct her own manuscript paper for this purpose.

A. Group 1

Name ______________________________

HOO, HOO!

Ethel Crowninshield

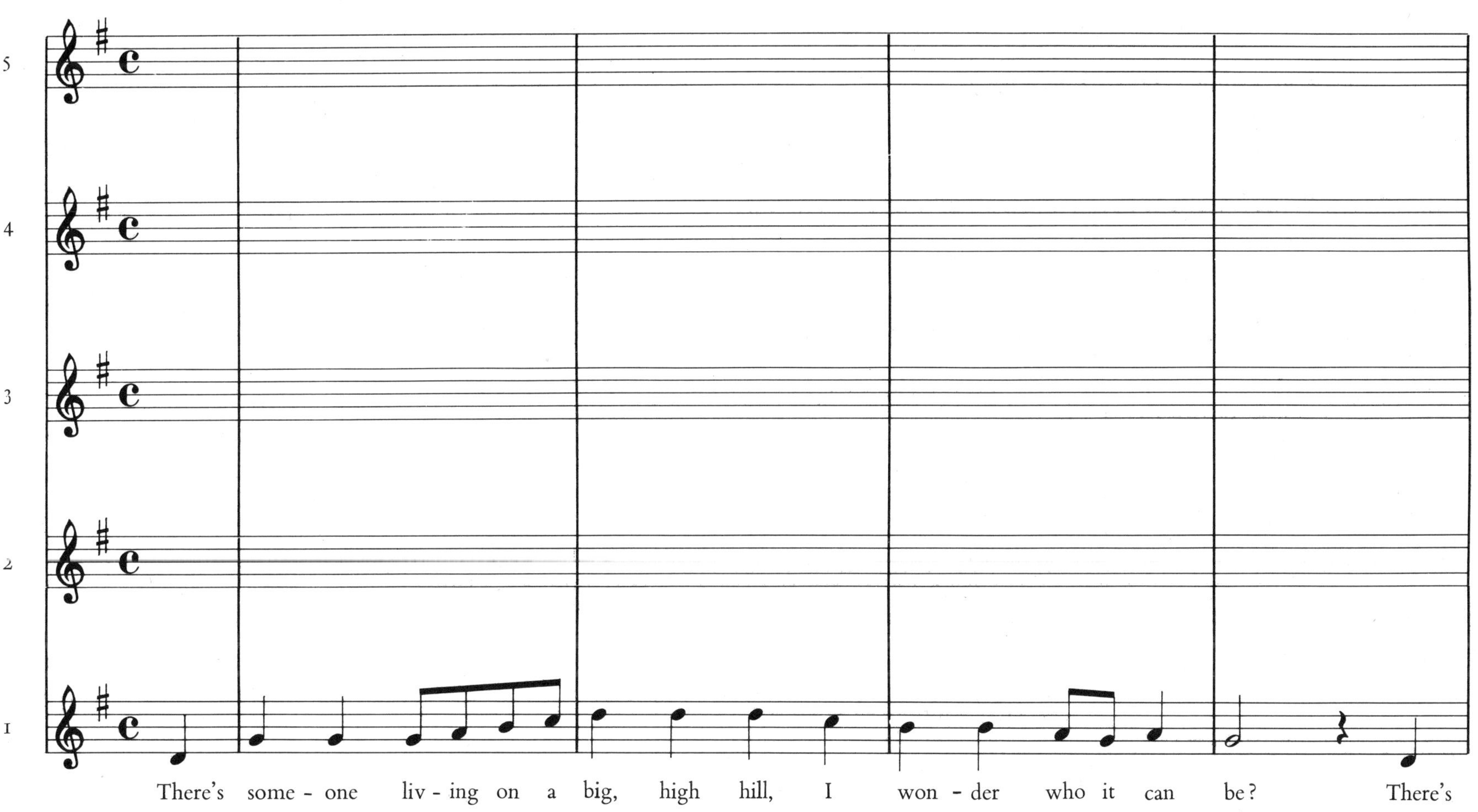

5
4
3
2
1
There's some - one liv - ing on a big, high hill, I won - der who it can be? There's

some - one liv - ing on a big, high hill, Who al - ways an - swers me. Hoo

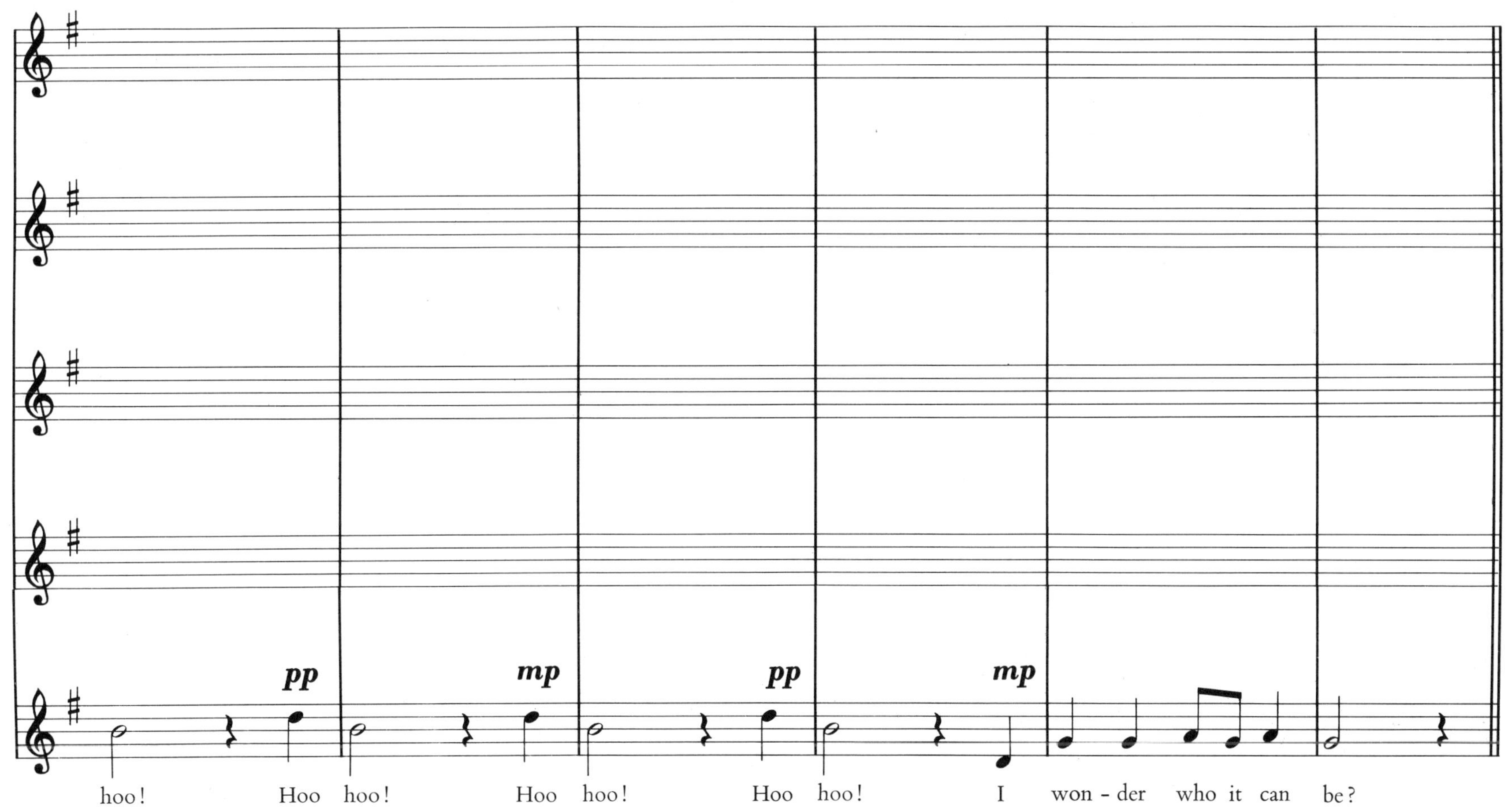
pp
mp
pp
mp
hoo! Hoo hoo! Hoo hoo! Hoo hoo! I won - der who it can be?

Name ____________________

THE OLD BRASS WAGON

American Folk Song

5
4
3
2
1
Cir - cle to the left, The old brass wa - gon, Cir - cle to the left, The old brass wa - gon,

Cir - cle to the left, The old brass wa - gon, You're the one my dar - ling.

Name ______________________________

MY NAME IS YON YONSON

Sweden

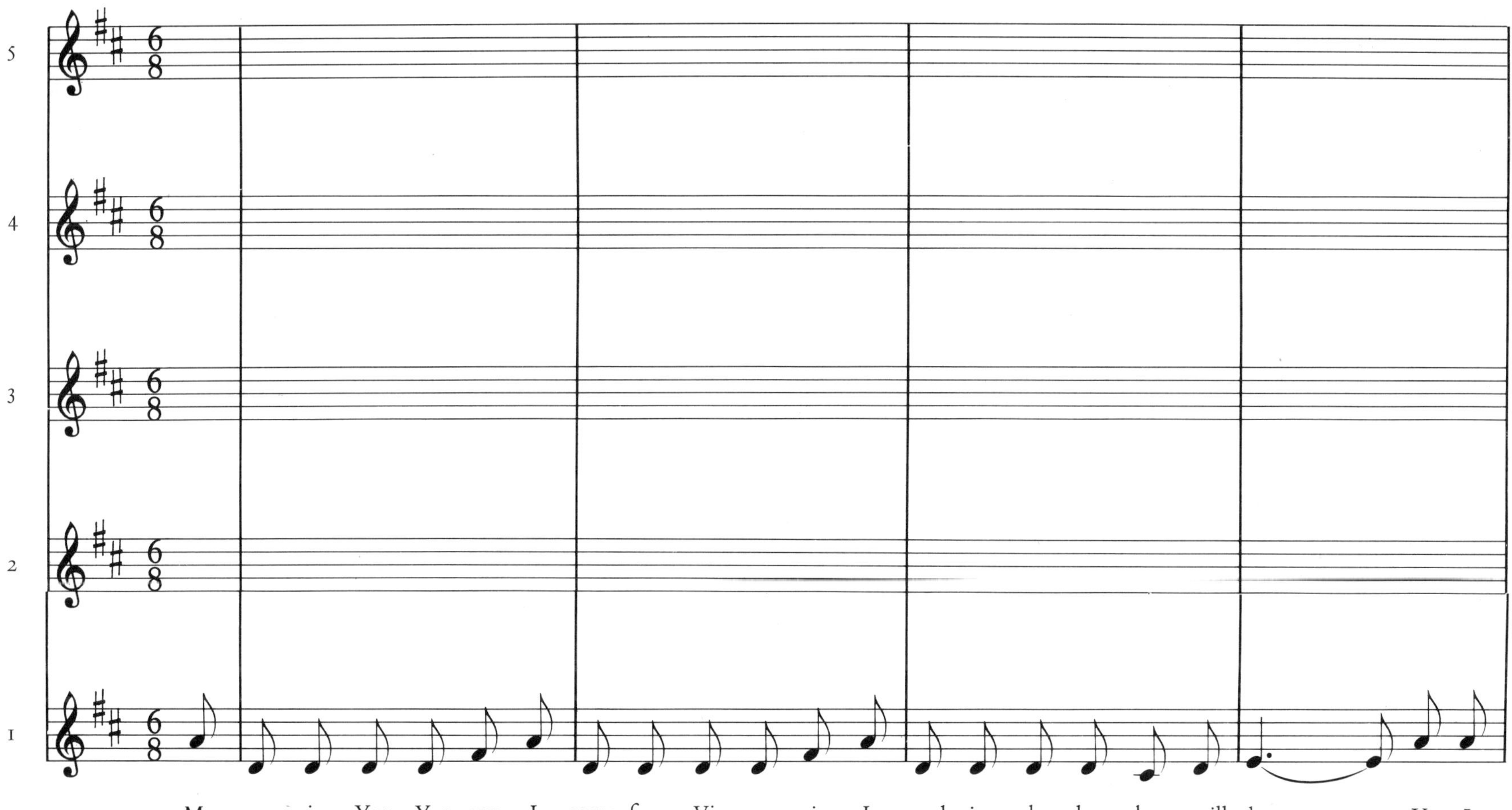
5
4
3
2
1
My name is Yon Yon-son, I come from Vis-con-sin, I vork in de lum-ber mill dere;____ Ven I

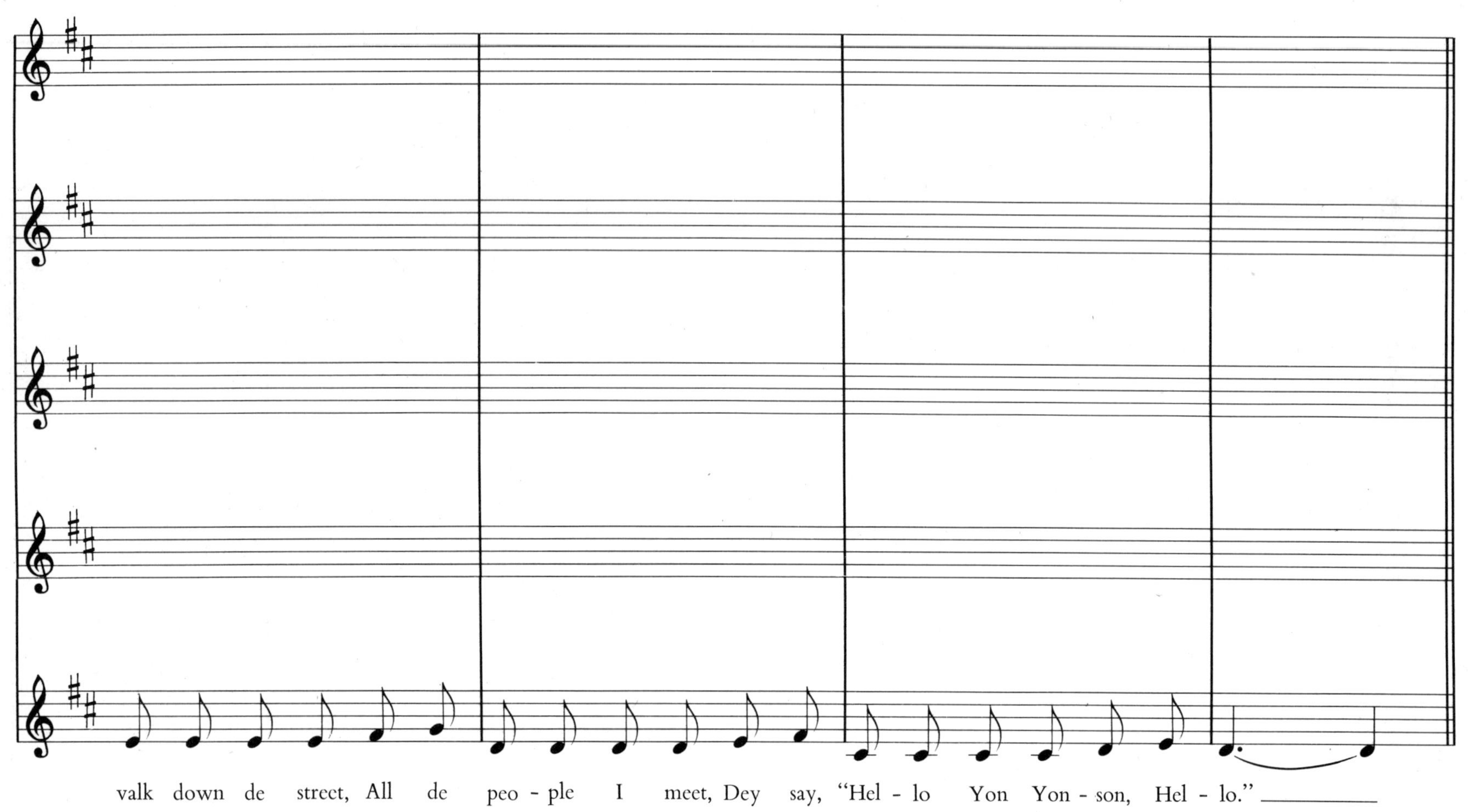
valk down de street, All de peo - ple I meet, Dey say, "Hel - lo Yon Yon - son, Hel - lo."

Name ____________________

THREE CORNERED HAT

American Camp Song

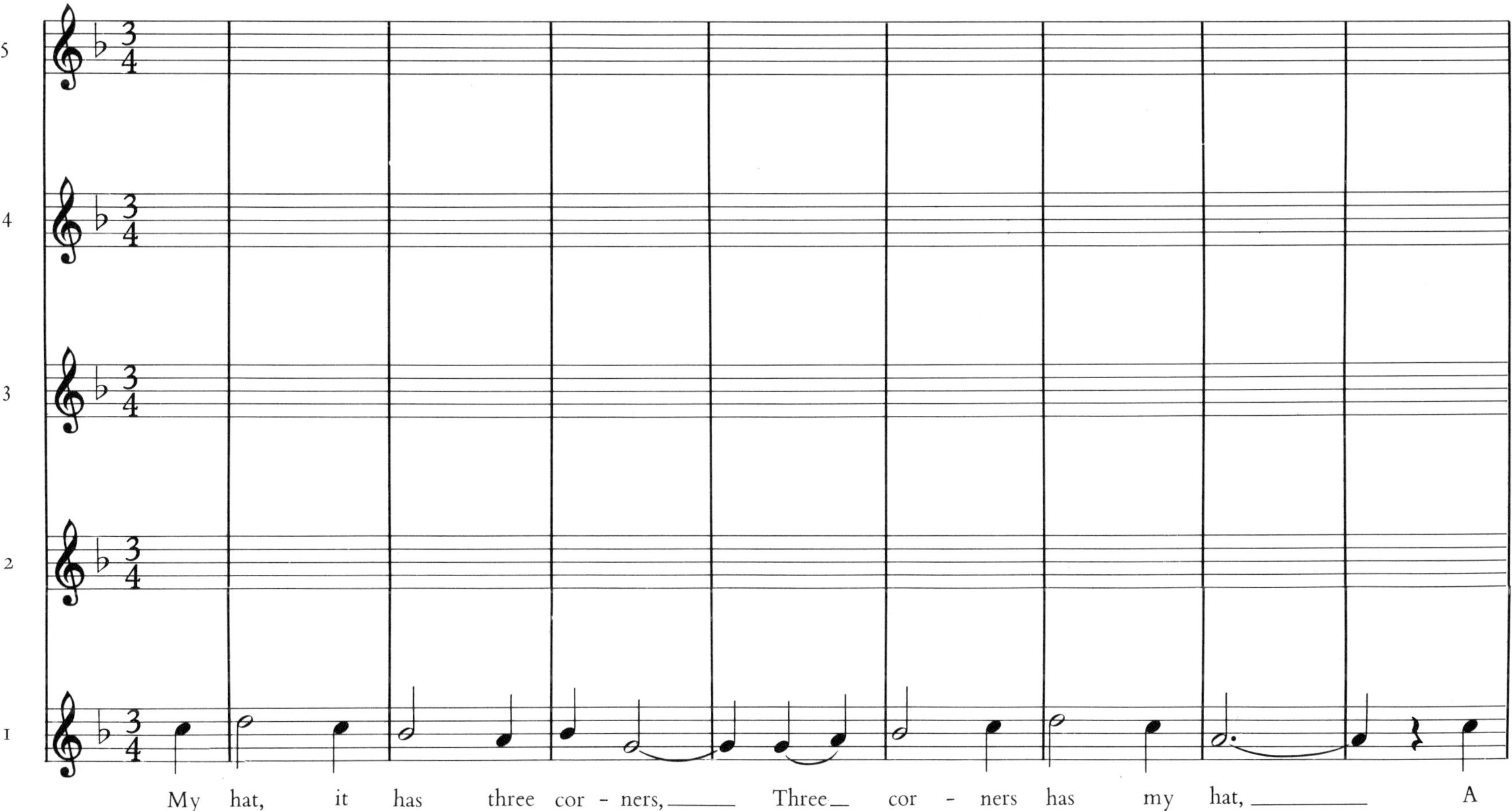
5
4
3
2
1
My hat, it has three cor - ners, Three cor - ners has my hat, A

hat with - out three cor - ners could nev - er be my hat.

Name ______________________________

TWINKLE, TWINKLE, LITTLE STAR

Nursery Tune

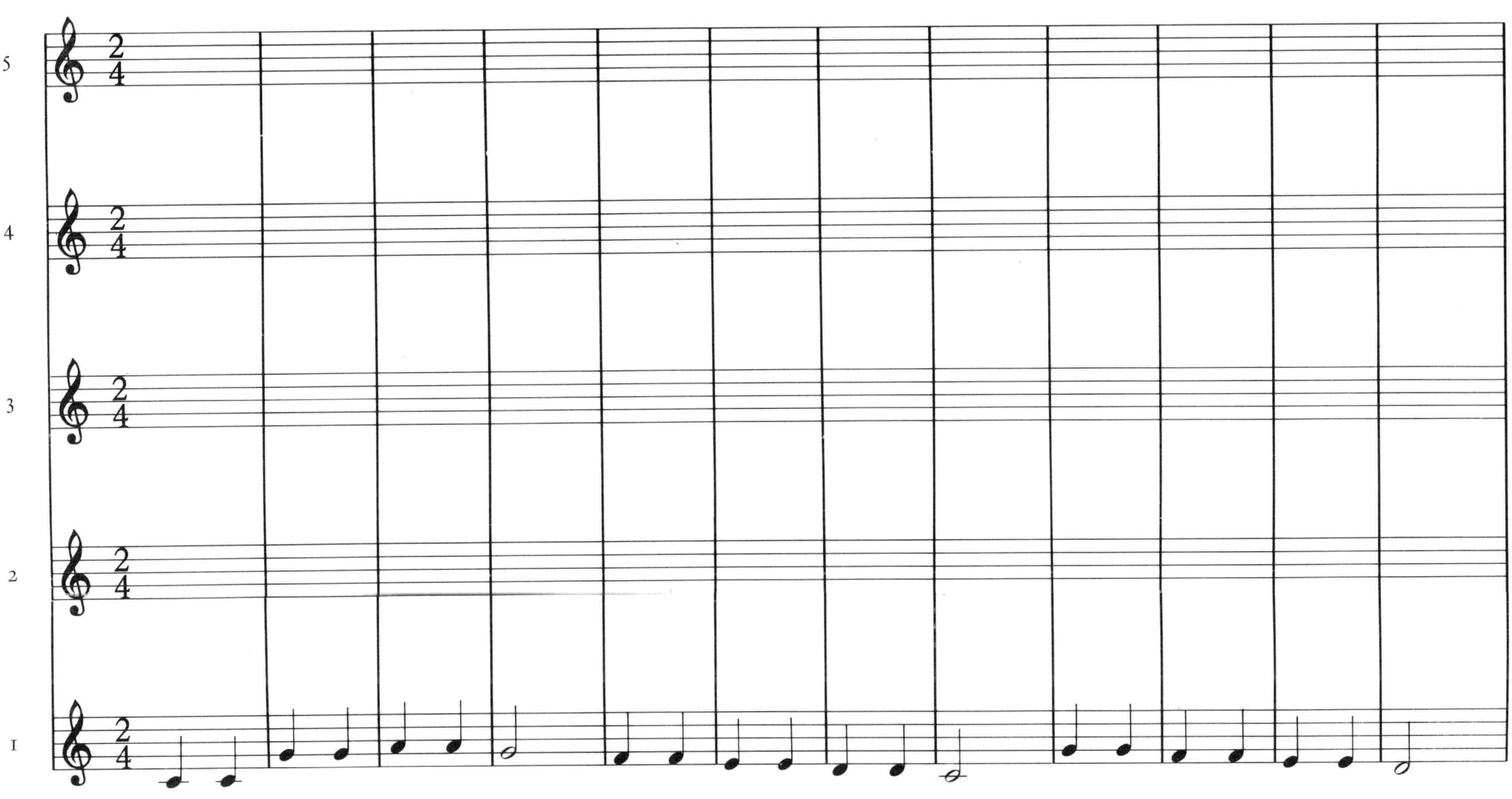
5
4
3
2
1
Twin-kle, twin-kle, lit - tle star, How I won-der what you are! Up a-bove the world so high,

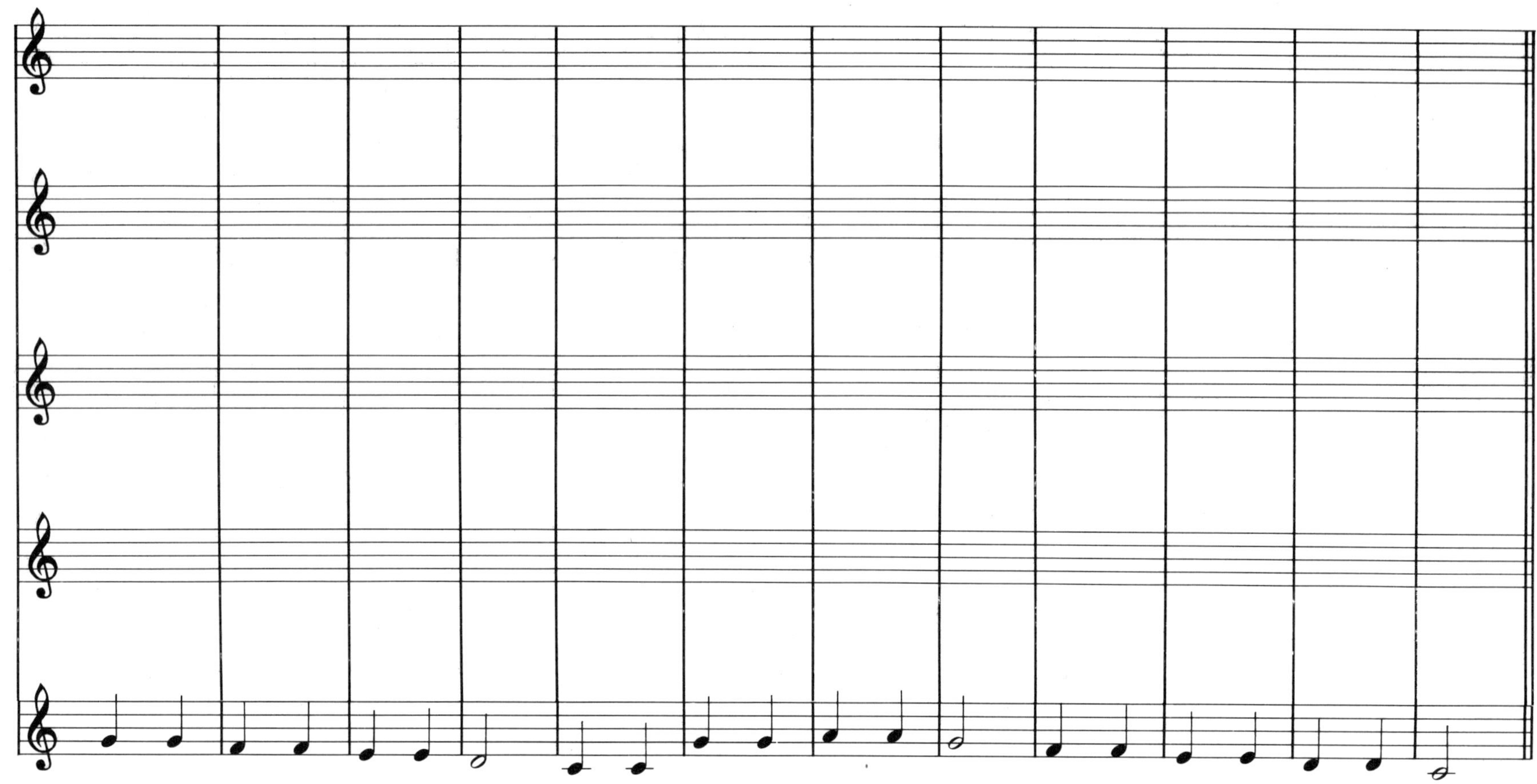
Like a dia - mond in the sky! Twin - kle, Twin - kle, lit - tle star, How I won - der what you are!

Name ______________________________

Name ______________________________

Name ______________________

Name ______________________________

Name ______________________

B. Group 2 *Name* ______________________

DOWN IN THE VALLEY

Kentucky Folk Song

Descant
Melody
Primary Harmony
Down in the val - ley, the val - ley so low, Hang your head o - ver, hear the wind

blow. Hear the wind blow, dear, hear the wind blow, Hang your head o - ver, hear the wind blow.

Name ______________________________

PAPER OF PINS

United States

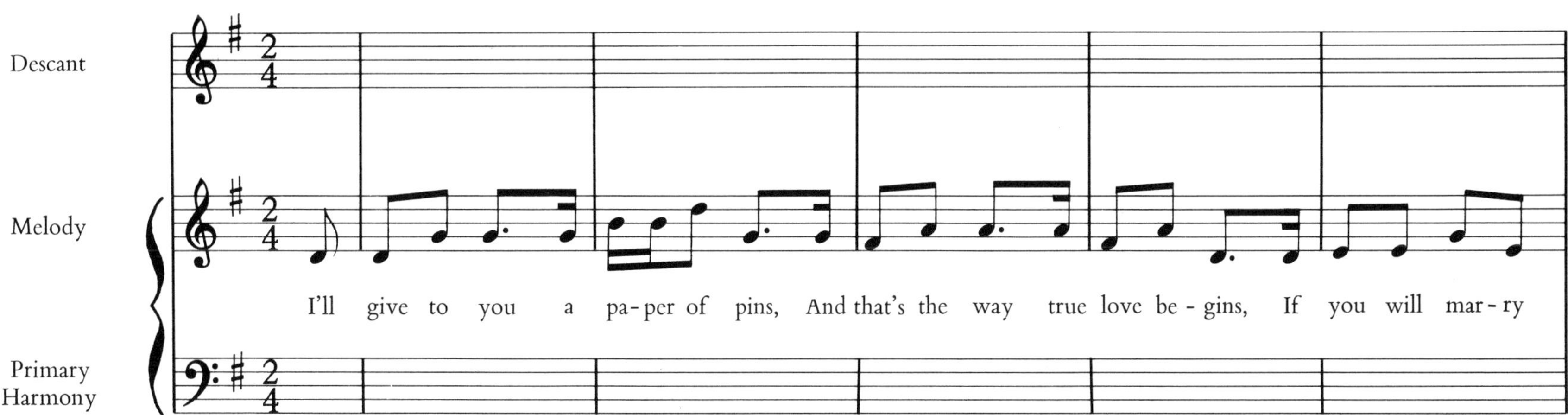
Descant
Melody
Primary Harmony
I'll give to you a pa-per of pins, And that's the way true love be - gins, If you will mar - ry

me, me, me, If you will mar - ry me.

Name ______________________________

HUSH, LITTLE BABY

United States

Descant
Melody
Primary Harmony
Hush lit - tle ba - by don't say a word, Dad-dy's gon-na buy you a mock - ing bird, And

if that mock - ing bird won't sing, Dad-dy's gon-na buy you a dia - mond ring.

German

Descant
Melody
Primary Harmony
Hop, hop, hop, Go and nev-er stop. When it's smooth and when it's storm-y,

Go a - long my lit - tle po - ny, Go and nev - er stop. Hop, hop, hop, hop, hop.

Name ________________________________

GOOD NIGHT

Round

Descant
Melody
Primary Harmony
Good night to you all, And sweet be thy sleep; May an - gels a -

round you their si - lent watch keep. Good night, Good night, Good night, Good night.

Name ______________________________

Name ______________________________

Name ______________________________

Name ______________________________

Name ______________________________

C. Group 3

Name ______________________________

A-HUNTING WE WILL GO

England

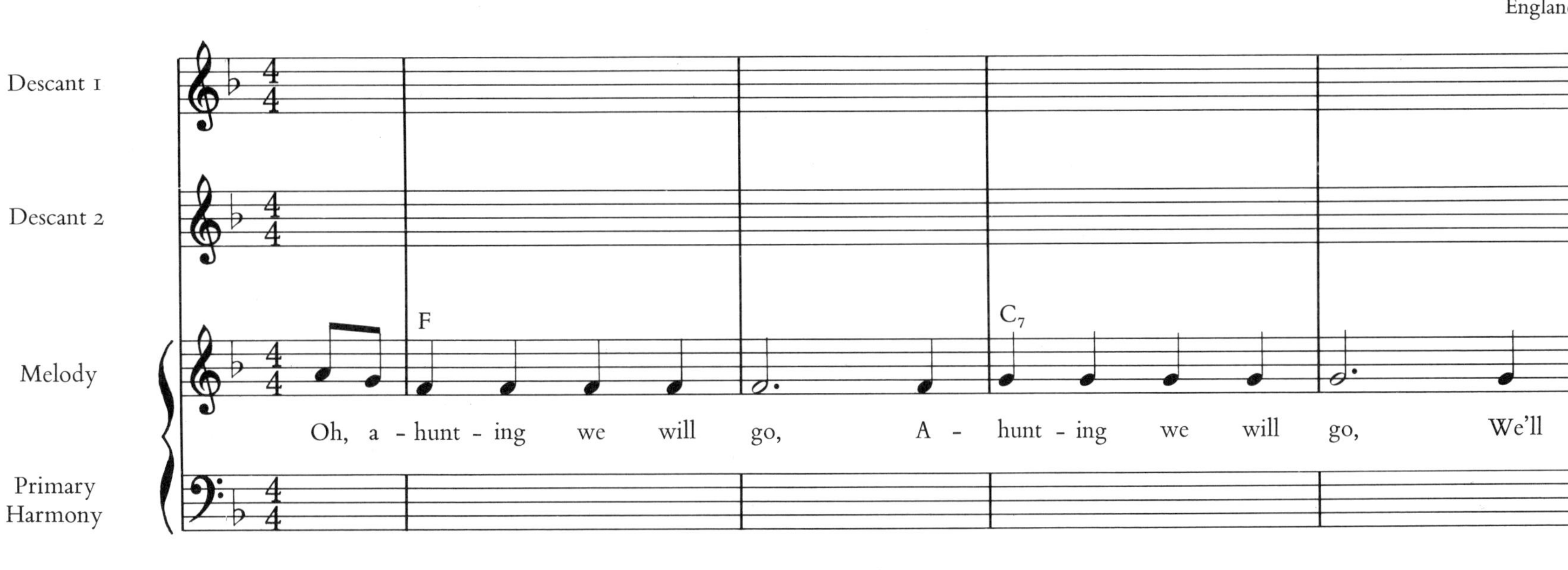

Descant 1
Descant 2
Melody
Primary Harmony
F
C7
Oh, a - hunt - ing we will go, A - hunt - ing we will go, We'll

F
B♭
F
C7
F
catch a lit - tle fox and put him in a box, And ne - ver let him go.

Name ______________________

BOBBY SHAFTO
England
Descant 1
Descant 2
Melody
Primary Harmony
Bob - by Shaf - to's gone to sea, Sil - ver buck - les on his knee;
He'll come back and mar - ry me,___ Pret - ty Bob - by Shaf - to!

Name ______________________________

THE WRAGGLE TAGGLE GYPSIES

England

Descant 1
Descant 2
Melody
Primary Harmony
There were three gyp - sies a - come to my door, And down - stairs ran this la - dy, O! The

first sang high, And the se - cond sang low, And the third sang bon-ny, bon - ny, Bis - cay, O!

Name ____________________

I SAW THREE SHIPS

English Christmas Carol

Descant 1
Descant 2
Melody
Primary Harmony
I saw three ships come sail - ing in, On Christ - mas Day, on Christ - mas Day, I
saw three ships come sail - ing in, On Christ - mas Day in the morn - ing.

Name ______________________

AWAY IN A MANGER

Words by Carl Muller   Music by Martin Luther

Descant 1
Descant 2
Melody
Primary Harmony
A - way in a man - ger, no crib for a bed, The lit - tle Lord

Je - sus laid down his sweet head. The stars in the sky looked

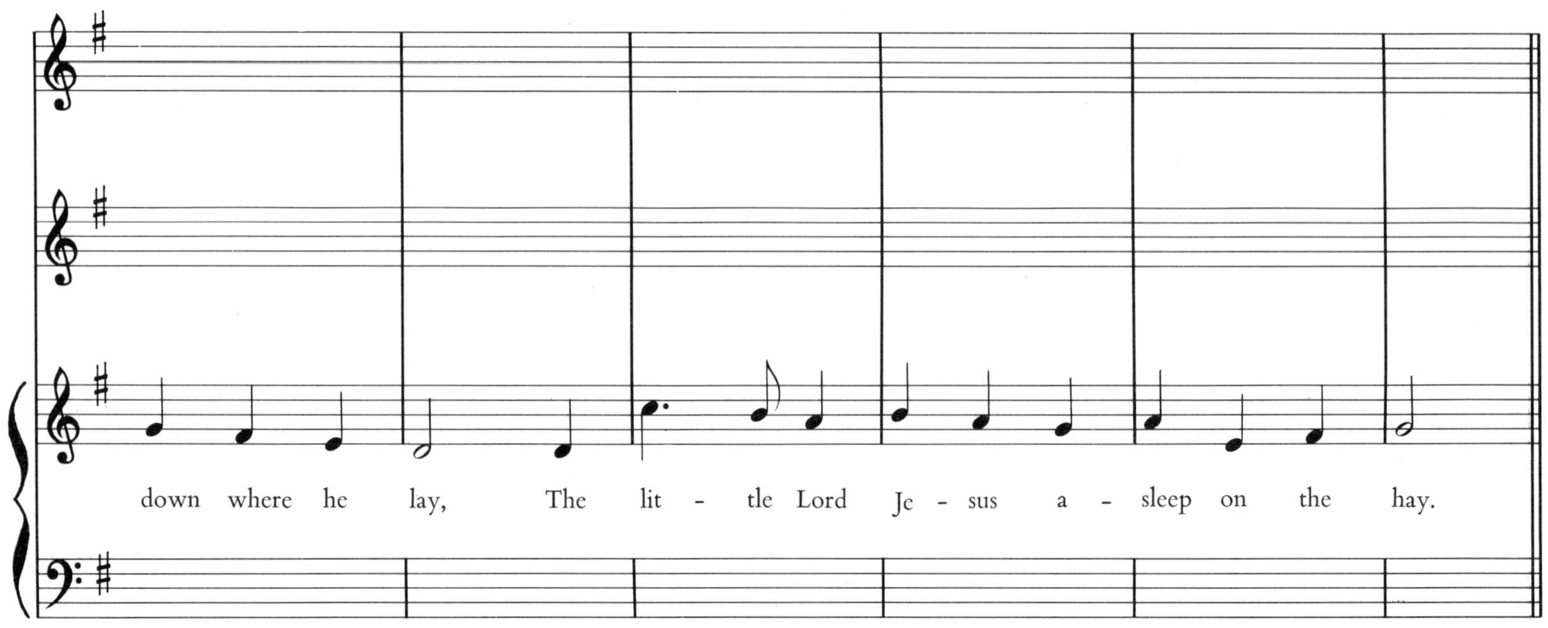
down where he lay, The lit - tle Lord Je - sus a - sleep on the hay.

Name ______________________________

Name ______________________________

Name ______________________________

Name ______________________________

Name ______________________

(name of selection)

(instrument)

(name of selection)

(instrument)

(name of selection)

(instrument)

(name of selection)

(instrument)

(name of selection)

(instrument)

(name of selection)

(instrument)

(name of selection)

(instrument)

(name of selection)

(instrument)

(name of selection)

(instrument)

(name of selection)

(instrument)

(name of selection)

(instrument)

(name of selection)

(instrument)

(name of selection)

(instrument)

(name of selection)

(instrument)

(name of selection)

(instrument)

(name of selection)

(instrument)

(name of selection)

(instrument)

(name of selection)

(instrument)

(name of selection)

(instrument)

(name of selection)

(instrument)

Part 3

HARMONIC ACCOMPANIMENT

1 Theory and Analysis

Elementary school-age children should have the experience of both hearing and participating in musical activities embracing all three elements of music: rhythm, melody, and harmony. Now that the student has had experience creating rhythmic and melodic orchestrations, the third, and final element —harmony—will be considered.

The purpose of this part is to teach the procedure for creating harmonic accompaniments. Since many elementary school music books do not provide harmonic accompaniments for melodies to be sung and/or played by the children, the creation of chordal support for these melodic and rhythmic activities must be assumed by the teacher. This part will deal with only three instruments which can be used to achieve vertical sonority: the autoharp, the ukulele, and the piano.

A. Definition of Harmonic Accompaniment

Melodies performed as separate entities can be beautiful and exciting experiences for both the performer and the listener. Indeed, unison performances should be a part of the total musical experience of children. However, all tunes or melodies do imply some kind of harmonic ingredients, and this was indicated in the part on Melody. The harmonic ingredients should be so structured that they enhance and broaden the effectiveness of the melody. If the harmonic material draws attention to itself, then it ceases to serve its main function, namely, to accompany.

The term HARMONIC ACCOMPANIMENT means a type, or pattern, of tones of primary harmonies. When arranged for the above instruments, they should be in keeping with the nature and peculiarities of each instrument.

B. Technical Suggestions and Accompaniment Patterns

1 Autoharp and Ukulele

Each string on the autoharp is tuned to its counterpart on the piano keyboard. The following chart is strategically placed at the base of the autoharp for this purpose:

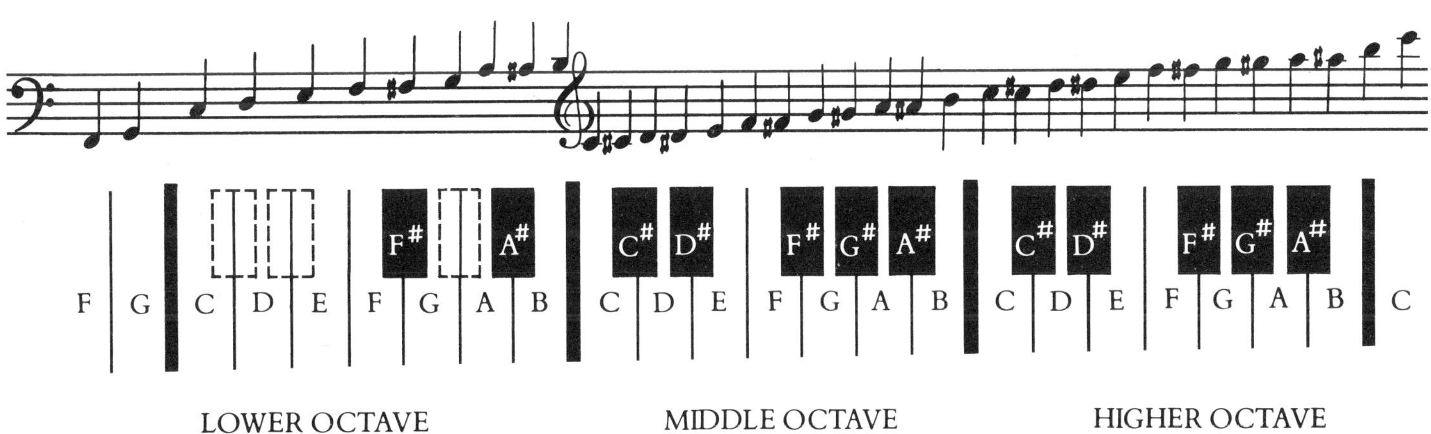
F#
A#
C#
D#
F#
G#
A#
C#
D#
F#
G#
A#
F
G
C
D
E
F
G
A
B
C
D
E
F
G
A
B
C
D
E
F
G
A
B
C
LOWER OCTAVE
MIDDLE OCTAVE
HIGHER OCTAVE

The most common tuning of the tenor ukulele is A, D, F♯, and B:

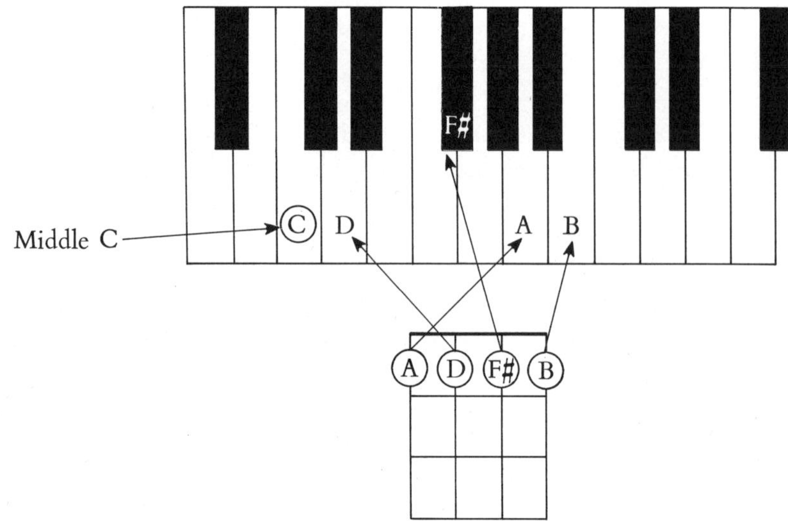

F♯
Middle C
C
D
A
B
A
D
F♯
B

Although there is little similarity in the construction of the autoharp and ukulele, the techniques of scoring their accompaniment patterns are sufficiently similar to group these two instruments together in this discussion. Sounds are produced on both instruments by "stroking" across the strings. The autoharp has several bars placed across the strings which, when pressed down separately, produce different chords when the strings are stroked. The ukulele requires the placing of the fingers of the left hand on certain frets to achieve the desired chord when the strings are stroked with the right hand. Our concern is to show how these strokes and chords are scored.

Symbols denoting the chord(s) to be played on the autoharp at a given point are indicated simply by the name of that particular chord. For instance, if the F chord is to be played—by pressing down the bar with this letter name on it with the *left hand* and stroking across the strings with the *right hand*, left to right—the resultant sound is the tones of the F chord: F-A-C.

Chord symbols for the ukulele are indicated by TABLATURES and/or chord letter names. To play chords, the four fingers of the left hand are placed in different positions on the frets, depending upon the particular chord to be sounded, and the right hand strokes across the strings. (A chart of tablatures for the tenor ukulele is found in Appendix B.)

The student must remember that these instruments, as well as all other chordal instruments, have as their primary function the providing of harmonic sonority for a given melody. With this in mind, it is suggested that the accompaniment be structured very simply.

In the song fragment below, stroke symbols are scored at certain places within the measure.

NOTE: It is not the purpose of this book to give detailed and lengthy discussion on "how to play" these instruments, no more than it purports to instruct persons in proper keyboard technique. Other books have been written with these objectives.

Melody
G
C
D7
AUTOHARP
UKULELE
G
C
D7

Only three strokes are suggested for this study. They are the *down* (\ ), *up* (/), and *down/up* (V). Normally, these types of strokes will suffice until the student has developed sufficient skill for advancement to more sophisticated strokes. The / and V are used more often on the ukulele than on the autoharp. The wide range of strings on the autoharp prohibits few departures from the \ stroke, unless some kind of special effect is sought.

The tempo and meter, along with the general characteristics of the melody, serve to indicate how many strokes should be effected per measure. A good rule of thumb to follow is: stroke according to the *meter rhythm*. This is especially true if the tempo of the piece is slow. If the selection is rather fast, or lively, then it would be feasible to have fewer strokes. As the student develops more skill in playing these instruments, variety can be achieved by syncopated strokes and variation in the intensity of the strokes.

2 *Piano*

The accompaniment patterns which the student will structure and score for the piano, in this book, will be designed only for the *left hand.* The right hand will reproduce the melody. The creative aspect of this endeavor lies principally in the fact that the student will score patterns commensurate with her keyboard skill.

NOTE: It should be kept in mind that "lots of notes" is no valid criterion for a good left hand piano accompaniment. It is much better, if one is to attempt to score for the piano, to score patterns that require minimal finger dexterity and keyboard skill. In this part the function of the piano, as well as of the autoharp and ukulele, is to provide chordal background and support. It would be very acceptable if the student played only the left hand and did not attempt to perform the melody and accompaniment simultaneously, provided that doing so would result in ineffectiveness.

Initially, the primary harmonies will be structured in *playing position.* Playing position (discussed in the part on Melody) eliminates a great deal of awkwardness in fingering. The example below, in C major, shows fingerings that are applicable in all keys, both major and minor.

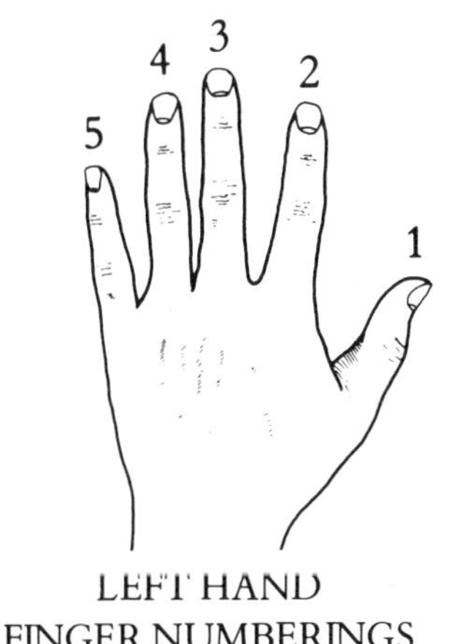

5
4
3
2
1

LEFT HAND
FINGER NUMBERINGS

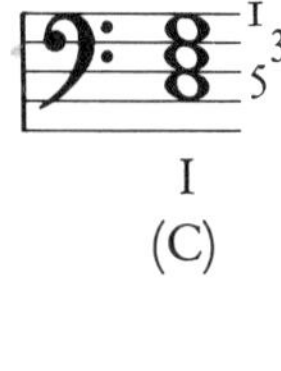

1
3
5

I
(C)

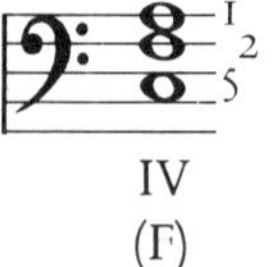

1
2
5

IV
(F)

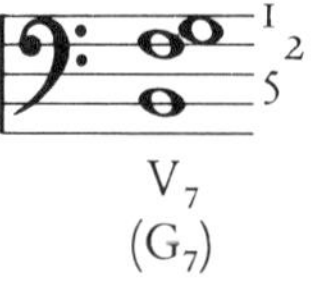

1
2
5

V_7
(G_7)

C. Procedure for Orchestrating Harmonic Accompaniments

Just as it was essential to determine the chord structure of melodies when evolving descants, or additional melodies, so it is necessary to determine the chord structure when creating harmonic accompaniments. The same procedure for determining chord structure is to be followed here.

1 *Autoharp and Ukulele*

When a melody has been analyzed harmonically, the student should determine how many "strokes" per measure are desired. The following factors should be kept in mind during this process: tempo, melodic rhythmic notation, and harmonic rhythm.

Tempo. As has been suggested before, if the piece is slow, stroking to *meter rhythm* is a valid and workable criterion. This will also suffice if the piece is considerably faster, although a reduction in the number of strokes per measure may be more practical, depending upon the student's performance skill.

To accompany the following song in meter rhythm would require four strokes per measure. Since the song moves along rather fast, two strokes might be more appropriate and, in fact, easier. Scoring for only one stroke per measure would also be acceptable.

SUR LE PONT D'AVIGNON

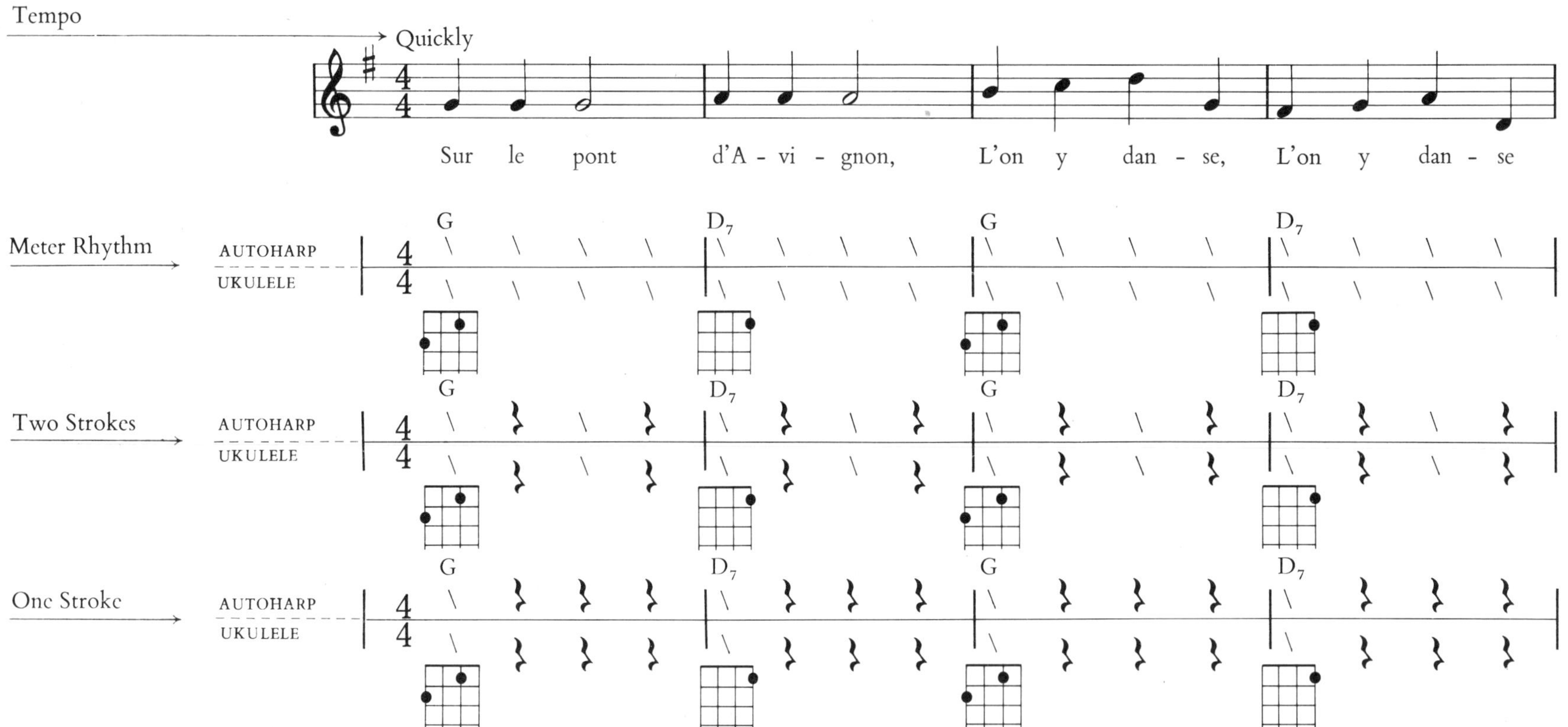
Tempo
Quickly
Sur le pont d'A - vi - gnon, L'on y dan - se, L'on y dan - se
Meter Rhythm
Two Strokes
One Stroke
AUTOHARP
UKULELE
G
D7
G
D7

Meter rhythm stroking is much more advisable when the tempo of the piece to be performed is indicated as quite slow or, as in the following example, "Reverently." This kind of stroking keeps the rhythm of the selection moving along steadily and elicits group rapport effectively.

AMERICA THE BEAUTIFUL

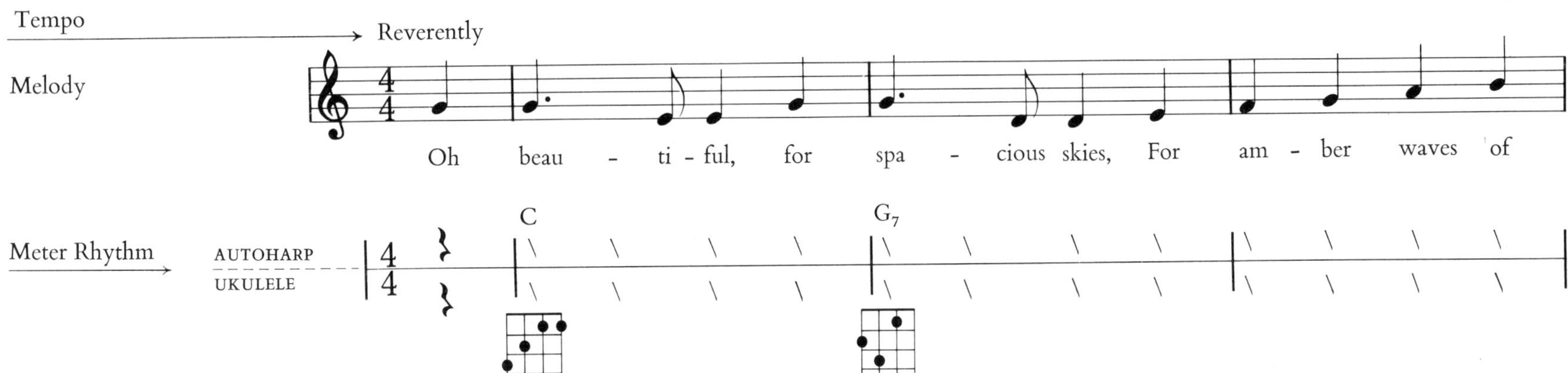

Tempo
Reverently
Melody
Oh beau - ti - ful, for spa - cious skies, For am - ber waves of
C
G7
Meter Rhythm
AUTOHARP
UKULELE

Melodic Rhythmic Notation. When the rhythmic notation of the melodic line is subdivided from its basic "beat note" (M.R.), it is suggested that the ukulele, especially, be scored to accentuate this rhythmic variety. The autoharp, as a general rule, should *not* be scored to stroke in less diminutive patterns than called for by the meter rhythm. However, in certain cases, where special effects are desired, this rule can be broken. The following example shows a subdivision of the beat note for the ukulele, with the autoharp stroking M.R.

HOW DO YOU DO?

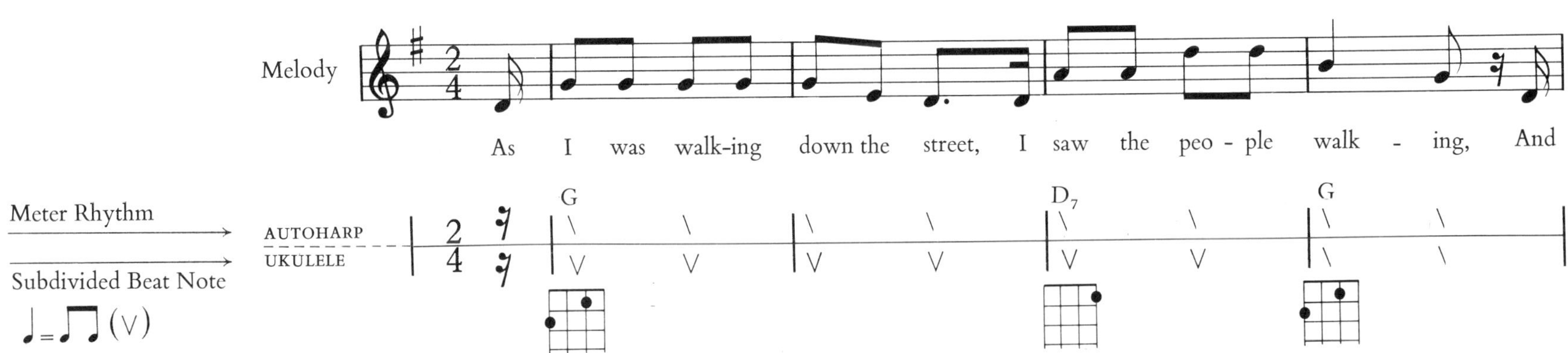

Melody
As I was walk-ing down the street, I saw the peo - ple walk - ing, And
G
D7
G
Meter Rhythm
AUTOHARP
UKULELE
Subdivided Beat Note
(V)

Harmonic Rhythm. Some melodies require more than one chord change within each measure. Since this change in sonority must be heard, the accompanying instruments must stroke them. *Tempo* and *melodic rhythm* are factors which still need to be considered. The example below shows a basic two-stroke-per-measure pattern on both the autoharp and ukulele which accommodates both the harmonic rhythm and the steady flow pronounced by the rhythm of the melody.

GO TELL AUNT RHODY

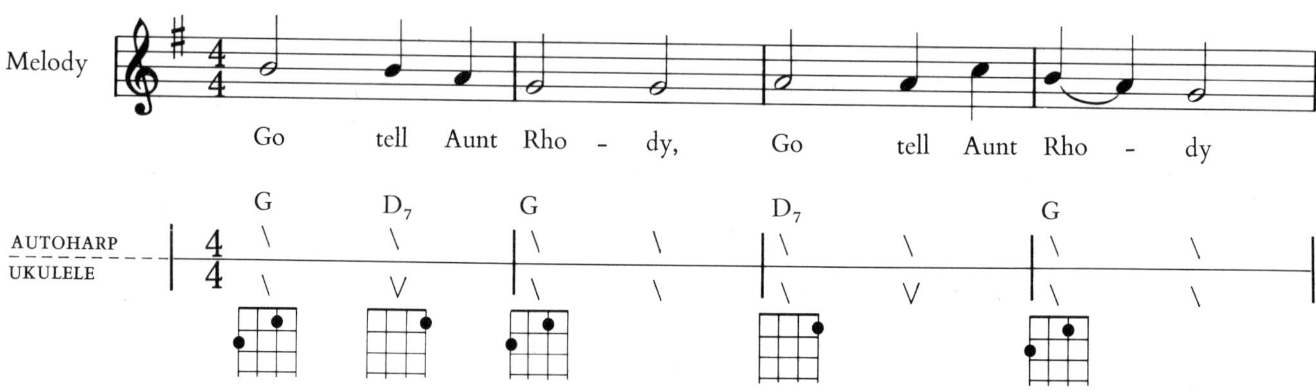
Melody
Go tell Aunt Rho - dy, Go tell Aunt Rho - dy
G D7 G D7 G
AUTOHARP
UKULELE

Most elementary school tunes are harmonized in such a way that only one chord per measure is necessary. Some change harmonies more often. In scoring for the accompaniment instruments, be sure to make such changes on the accompaniment staff and in the left hand of the piano score.

2 *Piano*

The limitation of accompaniment activity to the left hand is felt to be prudent and practical. Further, reducing all patterns to a minimum of rhythmic activity will increase confidence on the part of the novice keyboard practitioner, and instill in her a greater desire to utilize this exceptionally fine instrument to accompany future classroom activities.

The procedure for creating harmonic accompaniments for the piano (left hand) necessitates consideration of those same factors reviewed for the autoharp and the ukulele—tempo, melodic rhythmic notation, and harmonic rhythm. Following are examples of different types of accompaniment patterns. Examples 1–6 are based on the tune "Go Tell Aunt Rhody."

In this type of accompaniment the primary harmonies have been used once each measure, except where the harmony changes in measure 1. They are notated to consume a measure. This type of accompaniment is referred to as *harmonic rhythm:*

Example 1

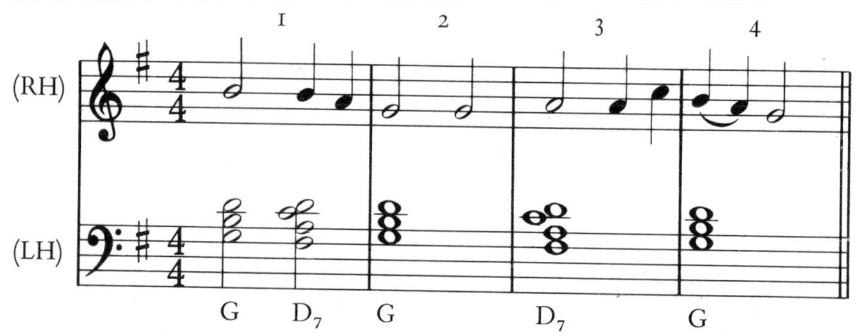
1 2 3 4
(RH)
(LH)
G D7 G D7 G

This accompaniment is *chord-type meter rhythm*, where the chords have been repeated to coincide with the *meter rhythm:*

Example 2

(RH)
(LH)
G D7 G D7 G

This accompaniment is *broken chord meter rhythm*, where one note of the chord is struck and then the rest of the chord is struck. Again the accompaniment is notated to coincide with the meter rhythm:

Example 3

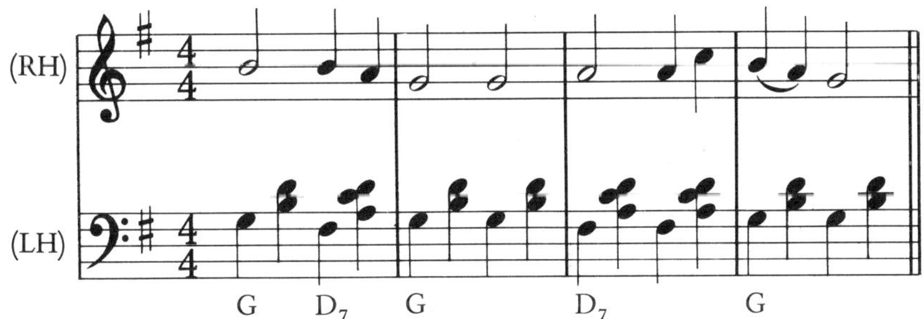
(RH)
(LH)
G D7 G D7 G

This is a *variation of the broken chord meter rhythm* illustrated in Example 3. Here, one note is struck with the same note an octave below, and then the entire chord is struck:

Example 4

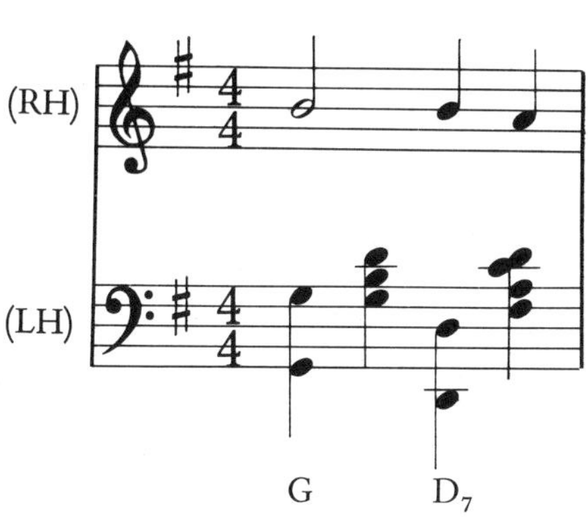
(RH)
(LH)
G D7

This accompaniment consists of *broken chord diminutive rhythm,* where eighth notes have been used instead of quarter notes:

Example 5

(RH)
(LH)
G
D7
G
D7
G

This accompaniment is an example of the use of *arpeggio,* where the chords are broken up into "running notes":

Example 6

(RH)
(LH)
G
D7
G
D7
G

Additional examples:

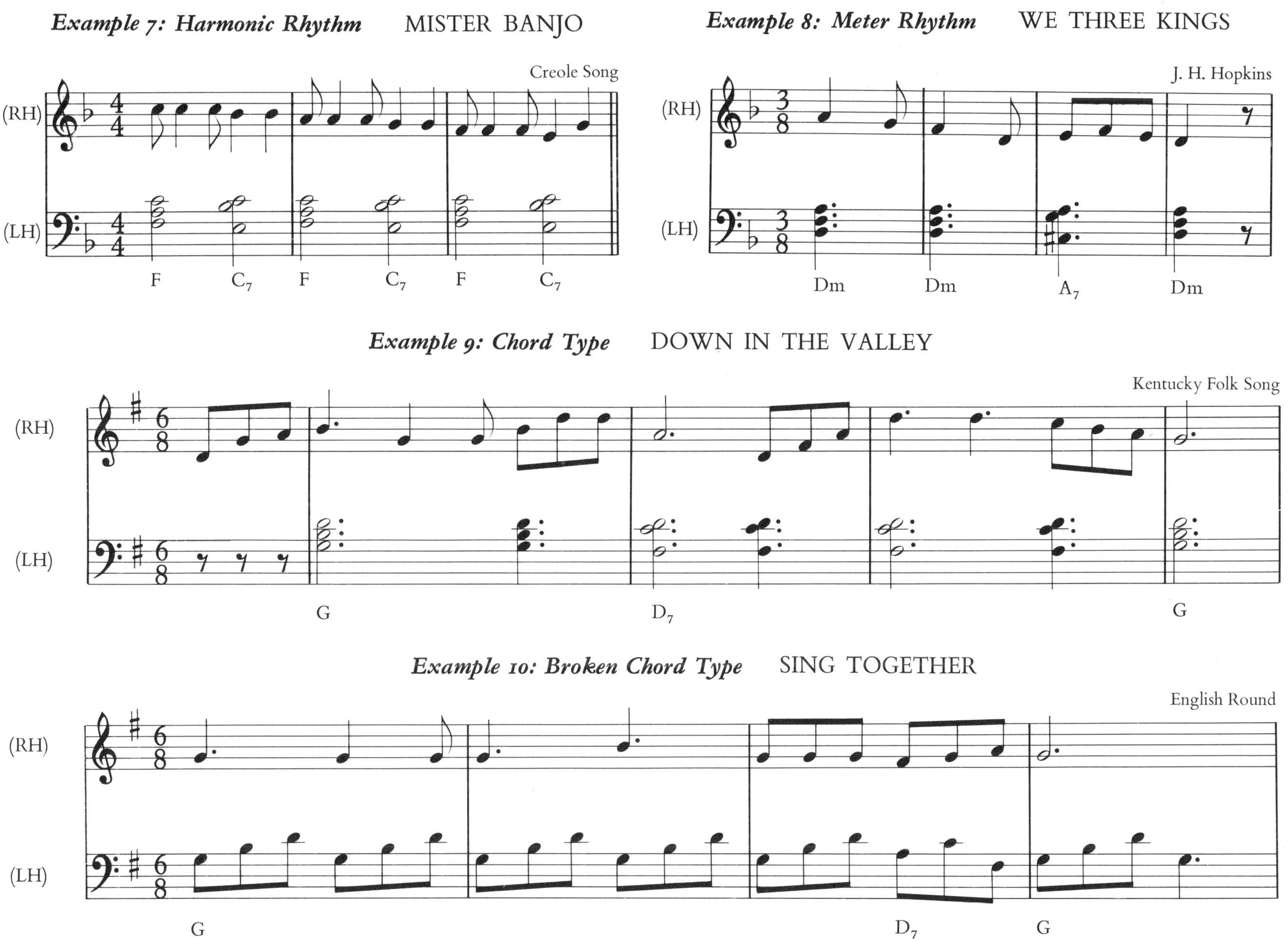
Example 7: Harmonic Rhythm
MISTER BANJO
Creole Song
(RH)
(LH)
F C7 F C7 F C7
Example 8: Meter Rhythm
WE THREE KINGS
J. H. Hopkins
(RH)
(LH)
Dm Dm A7 Dm
Example 9: Chord Type
DOWN IN THE VALLEY
Kentucky Folk Song
(RH)
(LH)
G D7 G
Example 10: Broken Chord Type
SING TOGETHER
English Round
(RH)
(LH)
G D7 G

Another way of structuring an accompaniment is to use a chord-type accompaniment that employs the rhythmic structure which is characteristic of the melody rhythm. (See the discussion of characteristic rhythms (C.R.'s) in the part on Rhythm.) The example below, using the same tune as Example 8, is structured by using the C.R. of measure 1:

Example 11: Characteristic Rhythm WE THREE KINGS

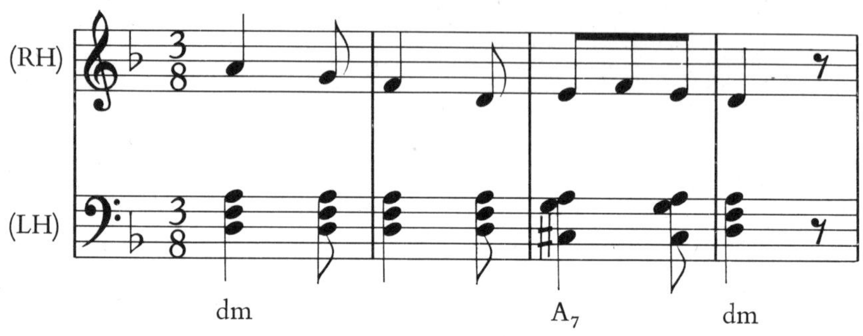
(RH)
(LH)
dm
A_7
dm

Characteristic
Rhythm

The student should observe that the preceding examples illustrated several types of patterns which could be structured for easy realization at the keyboard. Further, each example is simply a rhythmic variation on the primary harmonies in *playing position*.

2 Application

This section includes examples of harmonic accompaniment orchestrations scored for autoharp, ukulele and piano.

GRANDMA JONES
North Carolina Mountain Song
PIANO
(RH)
(LH)
Grand - ma Jones said a cu - ri - ous thing, "Boys can whis - tle but girls must sing."
AUTOHARP
UKULELE
F
That is what I heard her say; 'Twas no long-er than yes - ter - day.
F

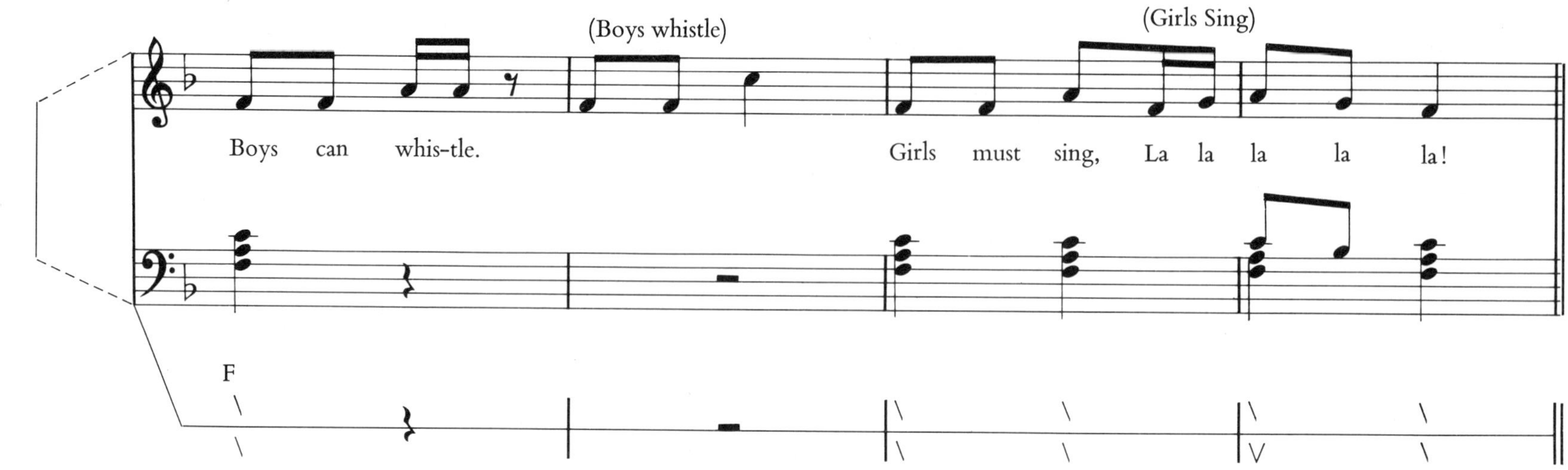
(Boys whistle)
(Girls Sing)
Boys can whis-tle.
Girls must sing, La la la la la!
F

CLEMENTINE

United States

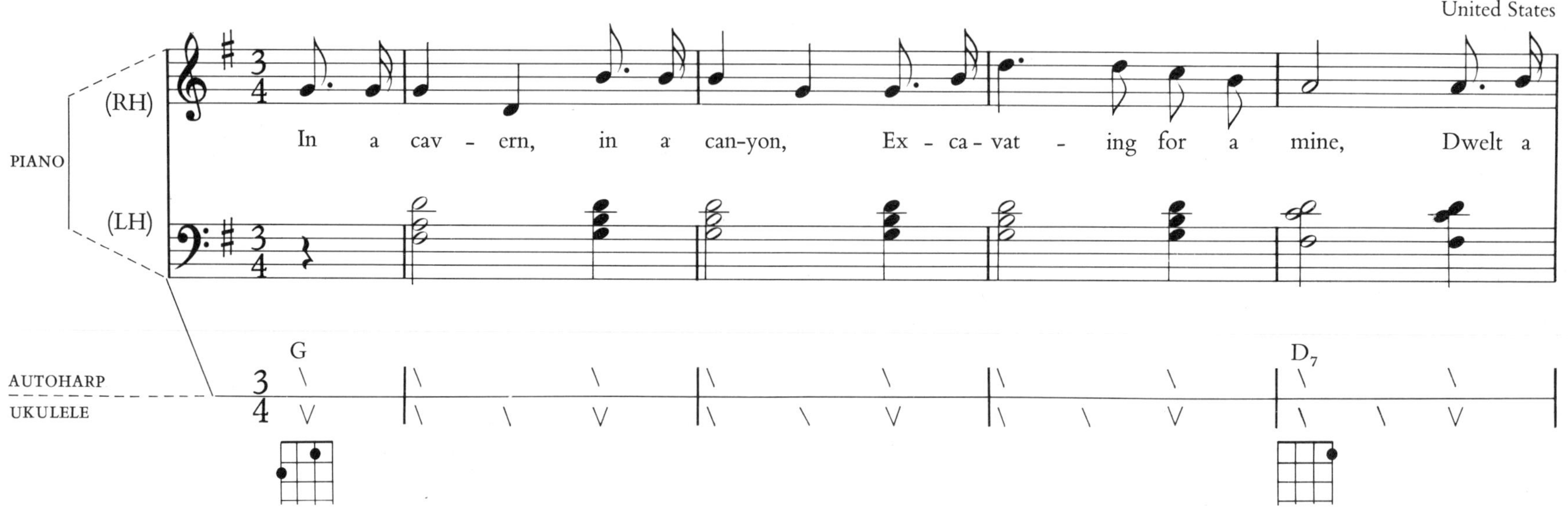
(RH)
(LH)
PIANO
In a cav - ern, in a can-yon, Ex - ca - vat - ing for a mine, Dwelt a
G
D7
AUTOHARP
UKULELE

min - er for - ty - nin - er, And his daugh-ter Clem-en - tine. Oh, my dar - ling, oh, my dar - ling, Oh, my
D7
G
D7
G
dar - ling Clem-en - tine! You are lost and gone for - ev - er, Dread-ful sor - ry Clem - en - tine!
G
D7
G
D7
G

THE DUCKLINGS

Traditional
Moderately
(RH)
(LH)
PIANO
AUTOHARP
UKULELE
All my lit - tle duck - lings, Swim - ming here and there;
C
F
C
Heads be - neath the wat - er, Tails up in the air.
G7
C
G7
C

AULD LANG SYNE

Robert Burns

PIANO
(RH)
(LH)
AUTOHARP
UKULELE
Should auld ac-quain-tance be for-got, And nev - er brought to mind? Should
F C7 F B♭
auld ac-quain-tance be for-got, And days of auld lang syne? For
F C7 dm C7 F

auld lang syne, my dear, For auld lang syne; We'll
F
C7
F
B♭
take a cup of kind - ness yet for auld lang syne.
F
C7
dm
C7
F

3 Assignments: Student Worksheets

Blank manuscript paper is included for the student to do additional harmonic accompaniments. The selection of material to be used is left to the discretion of the instructor and/or student.

The perforated sheets are included for the purpose of providing individual parts to members of the class performing assigned selections. The use of additional parts will require the student to construct her own manuscript paper for this purpose.

Name ____________________

THE PAW PAW PATCH

American Singing Game

(RH)
PIANO
(LH)
Pick-in' up paw paws, put 'em in the bas - ket, Pick-in' up paw paws, put 'em in the bas - ket,
AUTOHARP
UKULELE

Pick - in' up paw paws, put 'em in the bas - ket, 'Way down yon-der in the paw paw patch.

Name ______________________________

BLOW THE MAN DOWN

Old Chantey

(RH)
PIANO
(LH)
AUTOHARP
UKULELE
I'm go - ing to sing you a song of the sea, Hi, Ho, Blow the man down! And

all are in - vit - ed to join in with me, Give me some time to blow the man down.

Name ______________________

SILENT NIGHT

Franz Grüber

(RH)
PIANO
(LH)
AUTOHARP
UKULELE
Si - lent night! Ho - ly night! All is calm, all is bright.

Round yon vir - gin mo - ther and child, Ho - ly in - fant so ten - der and mild,

Sleep in heav - en - ly peace
Sleep in heav - en - ly peace.

Name ______________________________

GREENSLEEVES

England

(RH)
A - las! my love,— you do me wrong— To cast me off— dis - cour - teous-ly, And
PIANO
(LH)
AUTOHARP
UKULELE

I have lov - ed you so long,— De - light - ing in— your com - pan - y.

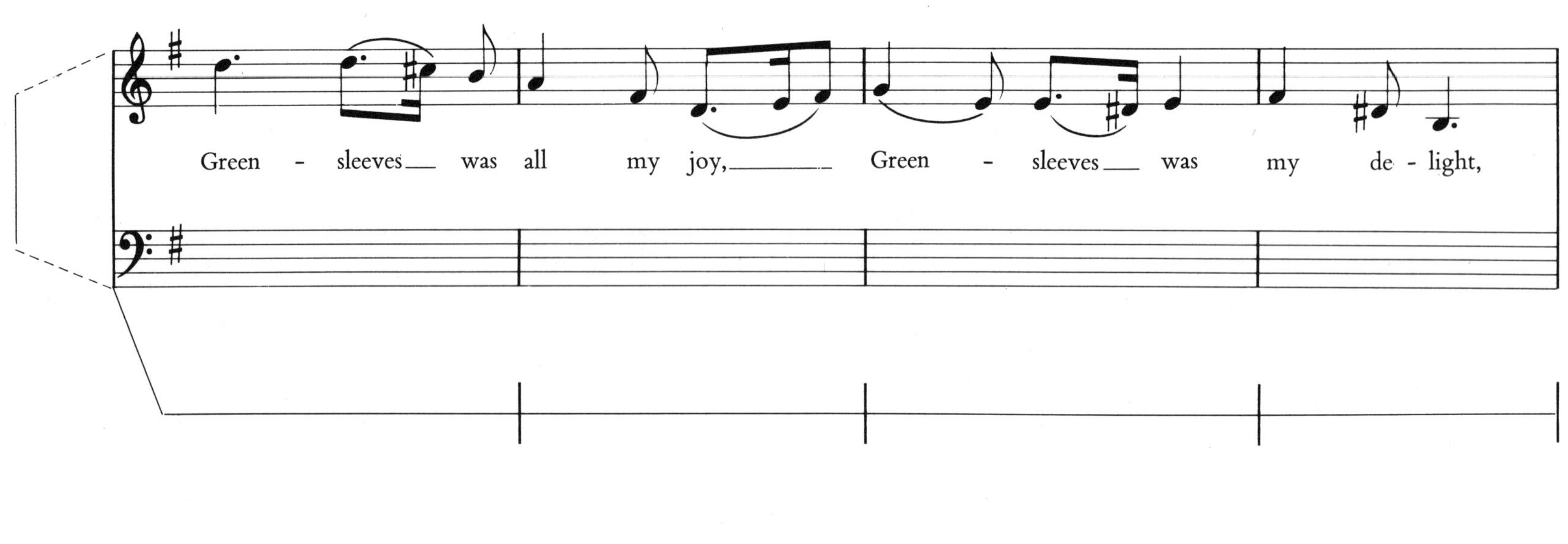
Green - sleeves was all my joy, Green - sleeves was my de - light,

Green - sleeves was my heart of gold, And who but my la - dy Green - sleeves.

Name ______________________________

OLD FOLKS AT HOME

Stephen Foster

(RH)
(LH)
PIANO
AUTOHARP
UKULELE
Way down up - on the Swa - nee Ri - ver, Far, far a - way,

There's where my heart is turn - ing ev - er, There's where the old folks stay.

All the world am sad and drear - y, Ev - 'ry - where I roam,
Oh! loved ones how my heart grows wear-y, Far from the old folks at home.

Name ______________________________

(RH)
PIANO
(LH)
AUTOHARP
UKULELE

Name ______________________________

(RH)
PIANO
(LH)
AUTOHARP
UKULELE

Name ________________________________

(RH)
PIANO
(LH)
AUTOHARP
UKULELE

Name ______________________________

(RH)
PIANO
(LH)
AUTOHARP
UKULELE

Name ______________________________

PIANO
(RH)
(LH)
AUTOHARP
UKULELE

(name of selection)

Autoharp

Ukulele

(name of selection)

Autoharp

Ukulele

(name of selection)

Autoharp

Ukulele

(name of selection)

Autoharp

Ukulele

(name of selection)

Autoharp
Ukulele

(name of selection)

Autoharp
Ukulele

(name of selection)

Autoharp
Ukulele

(name of selection)

Autoharp
Ukulele

(name of selection)

Autoharp

Ukulele

(name of selection)

Autoharp

Ukulele

(name of selection)

Autoharp

Ukulele

(name of selection)

Autoharp

Ukulele

(name of selection)

Autoharp

Ukulele

(name of selection)

Autoharp

Ukulele

(name of selection)

Autoharp

Ukulele

(name of selection)

Autoharp

Ukulele

(name of selection)

Autoharp

Ukulele

(name of selection)

Autoharp

Ukulele

(name of selection)

Autoharp

Ukulele

(name of selection)

Autoharp

Ukulele

Part 4

COMPLETED ORCHESTRATIONS

I Sample Orchestrations

The examples of completed orchestrations that follow have been scored to show three melodic activities (original melody plus two descants), three harmonic accompaniments (piano left hand, autoharp, and ukulele), and three different rhythm instruments (or sets of instruments). These completed scores allow for many possible varieties of classroom musical performances. Rhythmic, melodic, or harmonic activities can be sought individually or in combination with each other. It is suggested, however, that the children have the experience, at one time or another, of participating in and hearing "whole" orchestrations.

Suggestions for Performing Media

Following are some possible choices of instruments for specific types of musical activities. However, these are only *suggestions*, and any combination that produces worthwhile musical experiences for the children should be attempted.

RHYTHM

Since there is such an abundant number of possible rhythm instrument combinations, the following scores are only minimal suggestions. The use of many different types of instruments is the ultimate goal. While the children will develop desired motor skills through particular activities, they should also have the experience of hearing multiple combinations.

NOTE: The guiding criterion is to score for a particular instrument, or groups of instruments, the rhythmic pattern most commensurate with the physical structure of the instrument(s).

MELODY

Instrumental Descant: This melodic line can be performed by any kind of melody instrument, so long as the range of the melody does not exceed the limits of the particular instrument desired. *Tone bells* and *flutophones* are recommended.

Vocal Descant: As the name states, this melodic line can be sung, either with neutral syllables or with the same text as the original melody. It should be observed, however, that this melody might also be performed by instruments.

Original Melody (in piano score): The initial experience in performing the original melody should probably be vocal. Again, involve instrumentalists whenever advisable.

NOTE: The obvious result here is a three-part activity. Experiment with vocal and instrumental combinations *and* with combinations of all or one or the other.

HARMONY

As noted on the following scores, the *piano* (left hand), the *autoharp*, and the *ukulele* are suggested as instruments to provide the accompaniment and give aural perception of harmonic sonority. The *harmonia* and *guitar* can also be used, either as substitutions or additions.

FLOW GENTLY, SWEET AFTON

Words by Robert Burns Music by J. E. Spilman

Instrumental Descant
Vocal Descant
Flow gent - ly, sweet Af - ton, a - mong thy green braes, Flow gent - ly, I'll
PIANO
Flow gent - ly, sweet— Af - ton, a - mong thy green braes, Flow gent - ly, I'll
G D7 G C G D7
AUTOHARP UKULELE
Rhythm 1:
STICKS
Rhythm 2:
CLAVES
Rhythm 3:
WRIST BELLS

sing thee a song in thy praise; My Ma - ry's a - sleep by this
sing thee a song in thy praise; My Ma - ry's a - sleep by this
G
D7
G
D7
G

mur - mur - ing stream, Flow gent - ly, sweet Af - ton, dis - turb not her dream.
mur - mur - ing stream, Flow gent - ly, sweet Af - ton, dis - turb not her dream.
C
G
D7
G
D7
G
D7
G

JOSHUA FIT THE BATTLE OF JERICHO

Negro Spiritual

Instrumental Descant
Vocal Descant
Josh-ua fit the bat-tle of___ Jer-i-cho,___ Jer-i-cho,___ Jer-i-cho,___
PIANO
Josh-ua fit the bat-tle of___ Jer-i-cho,___ Jer-i-cho,___ Jer-i-cho,___
dm
gm
A7
AUTOHARP UKULELE
Rhythm 1: STICKS
Rhythm 2: WRIST BELLS
Rhythm 3: CLAVES

Josh-ua fit the bat-tle of Jer-i - cho, And the walls come tum-blin' down.
Josh-ua fit the bat-tle of Jer-i - cho, And the walls come tum-blin' down.
dm
A7
dm

You may talk a-bout your king of Gi - de - on,
You may talk a-bout your man of Saul,
There's
You may talk a-bout your king of Gi - de - on,
You may talk a-bout your man of Saul,
There's
dm
A7
dm
A7
dm
A7
dm
A7

none like good old Josh - ua, At the bat-tle of Jer - i - cho!
none like good old Josh - ua, At the bat-tle of Jer - i - cho!
dm A7 dm A7 dm A7 dm

THE CUCKOO

Austria
Instrumental Descant
Ho lay ah, Ho lay
Vocal Descant
Ho lay ah, Ree lee
PIANO
Oh, I went to the flow-ing spring, Where the wat - er's so
F
C7
F
C7
AUTOHARP
UKULELE
Rhythm 1:
STICKS
Rhythm 2:
SAND BLOCKS
Rhythm 3:
TAMBOURINE

ah, Ah ree lee ah,
ah, Ho lay ah, Ho lay ah ree lee ah, Ho lay ah,
blue, And I ho, lay a cuck-oo, Ho lay ah ree lee ah, Ho, lay a cuck-oo,
F
C7
F

Ho lay ho, Lay ah ree lee ah.
Ho lay ah ree lee ah, Ho lay ah ree lee ah.
Ho lay ah ree lee ah, Heard there the cuck-oo bird, As she sang clear and true.
C7
F

Ho lay ah, Ho lay ah, Ree lee ah.
Ho lay ah, Ho lay ah ree lee ah, ho lay ah Ho lay ah ree lee ah hoo.
Ho lay ah, Ho lay ah ree lee ah, Ho, lay ah cuck-oo, Ho lay ah ree lee ah hoo.
F
C7
shake

ARE YOU SLEEPING?

France

Instrumental Descant
Vocal Descant
Are you sleep - ing, are you sleep - ing, Broth - er John, Broth - er John?
PIANO
Are you sleep - ing, are you sleep - ing, Broth - er John, Broth - er John?
G
AUTOHARP
UKULELE
Rhythm 1:
STICKS
Rhythm 2:
CLAVES
Rhythm 3:
TOM TOM DRUM

Morn-ing bells are ring - ing, Morn-ing bells are ring - ing, Ding ding dong, Ding ding dong.
Morn-ing bells are ring - ing, Morn-ing bells are ring - ing, Ding ding dong, Ding ding dong.

JINGLE BELLS

United States

Instrumental Descant
Vocal Descant
Jin - gle bells, jin - gle bells, Jin - gle all the way! Oh, what fun it
PIANO
Jin - gle bells, jin - gle bells, Jin - gle all the way! Oh, what fun it
G
D7
AUTOHARP
UKULELE
Rhythm 1:
TRIANGLE
Rhythm 2:
WRIST BELLS
Rhythm 3:
STICKS

1.
2.
is to ride, In a one horse o - pen sleigh! Oh! one horse o - pen sleigh!
is to ride, In a one horse o - pen sleigh! Oh! one horse o - pen sleigh!
G
D7
D7
G

HOW DO YOU DO?

German Folk Tune

Instrumental Descant
Vocal Descant
As I was walk-ing down the street, I saw the peo-ple walk - ing; And when they met some-
PIANO
As I was walk-ing down the street, I saw the peo-ple walk - ing; And when they met some-
G
D7
G
G
AUTOHARP UKULELE
Rhythm 1:
STICKS
Rhythm 2:
TAMBOURINE
Rhythm 3:
CLAVES

one they knew, They start-ed in a - talk - ing: "How do you do?" ___ "How do you
one they knew, They start-ed in a - talk - ing: "How do you do?" ___ "How do you
D7
G
G
C
G
C
S
S

do?" And when they met some-one they knew, They start-ed in a-talk-ing.
do?" And when they met some-one they knew, They start-ed in a-talk-ing.
G
D7
G

CAMP TOWN RACES
Stephen Foster
Instrumental Descant
Vocal Descant
Doo-dah! Doo-dah! Doo - dah, doo - dah, doo - dah day!
PIANO
1. The Camp-town la - - dies
2. See them fly - ing on a
D
AUTOHARP
UKULELE
Rhythm 1:
WRIST BELLS
TRIANGLE
Rhythm 2:
TAMBOURINE
CLAVES
Rhythm 3:
STICKS

★ In 2/4 meter, the ukulele stroke markings, \ V, should be realized as ♪ ♬. That is, the down-beat \ , which is an eighth note, and the down-up stroke, which is a two-sixteenth note figure V. Refer to stroke markings discussed on page 235.

Doo - dah! Doo - dah!
sing this song, Doo - dah! Doo - dah! The Camp-town race - track five miles long,
ten - mile heat, Round the race - track then re - peat,
A7
D

Oh! doo - dah - day. Go'n' to run all night! Go'n' to run all
Oh! doo - dah - day. Go'n' to run all night! Go'n' to run all
A_7
D
D
G

day!
Some-bod-y bet on the bay.
day! I'll__ bet my mo-ney on the bob-tail nag, Some-bod-y bet on the bay.
D
A7
D

2 Supplementary Manuscript Paper

Blank manuscript paper is included here for the student to do additional orchestrations. The selection of material to be used is left to the discretion of the instructor and/or student.

The perforated sheets are included for the purpose of providing individual parts to members of the class performing assigned selections. Additional parts will require the student to construct her own manuscript paper for this purpose.

Name ______________________

Instrumental Descant

Vocal Descant

PIANO

AUTOHARP
UKULELE

Rhythm 1:

Rhythm 2:

Rhythm 3:

Name ___

Name ______________________

Instrumental Descant

Vocal Descant

PIANO

AUTOHARP
UKULELE

Rhythm 1:

Rhythm 2:

Rhythm 3:

Name ________________________________

Name ______________________

Instrumental Descant

Vocal Descant

PIANO

AUTOHARP
UKULELE

Rhythm 1:

Rhythm 2:

Rhythm 3:

Name ______________________________

Name ______________________

Instrumental Descant

Vocal Descant

PIANO

AUTOHARP
UKULELE

Rhythm 1:

Rhythm 2:

Rhythm 3:

Name ______________________________

Name ______________________________

Instrumental Descant

Vocal Descant

PIANO

AUTOHARP
UKULELE

Rhythm 1:

Rhythm 2:

Rhythm 3:

Name ______________________________

(name of selection)

Autoharp / Ukulele

(name of selection)

Autoharp / Ukulele

(name of selection)

Autoharp / Ukulele

(name of selection)

Autoharp / Ukulele

(name of selection)

Autoharp

Ukulele

(name of selection)

Autoharp

Ukulele

(name of selection)

Autoharp

Ukulele

(name of selection)

Autoharp

Ukulele

(name of selection)

Autoharp
Ukulele

(name of selection)

Autoharp
Ukulele

(name of selection)

Autoharp
Ukulele

(name of selection)

Autoharp
Ukulele

(name of selection)

Autoharp

Ukulele

(name of selection)

Autoharp

Ukulele

(name of selection)

Autoharp

Ukulele

(name of selection)

Autoharp

Ukulele

(name of selection)

Autoharp
Ukulele

(name of selection)

Autoharp
Ukulele

(name of selection)

Autoharp
Ukulele

(name of selection)

Autoharp
Ukulele

Appendix A

Summary of the Fundamentals of Music

It is felt that successful completion of this workbook does not necessitate an exhaustive and comprehensive recall of *all* of the many fundamental elements of music. Indeed, this book is based upon the premise that such success can be achieved with only a minimal background in music. Prior to or at the very beginning of this course of study, the completion of a Programmed Series in Music Fundamentals will give the student a broader base upon which to build creative experiences in rhythm, melody, and harmony. A thorough mastery of the following summary is suggested as a minimal prerequisite for handling the material in this workbook.

I Notation

1 ***Notes and Rests (with dotted notes derivations)***

The relative length of time consumed by pitch and silence is notated by the symbols in the chart below:

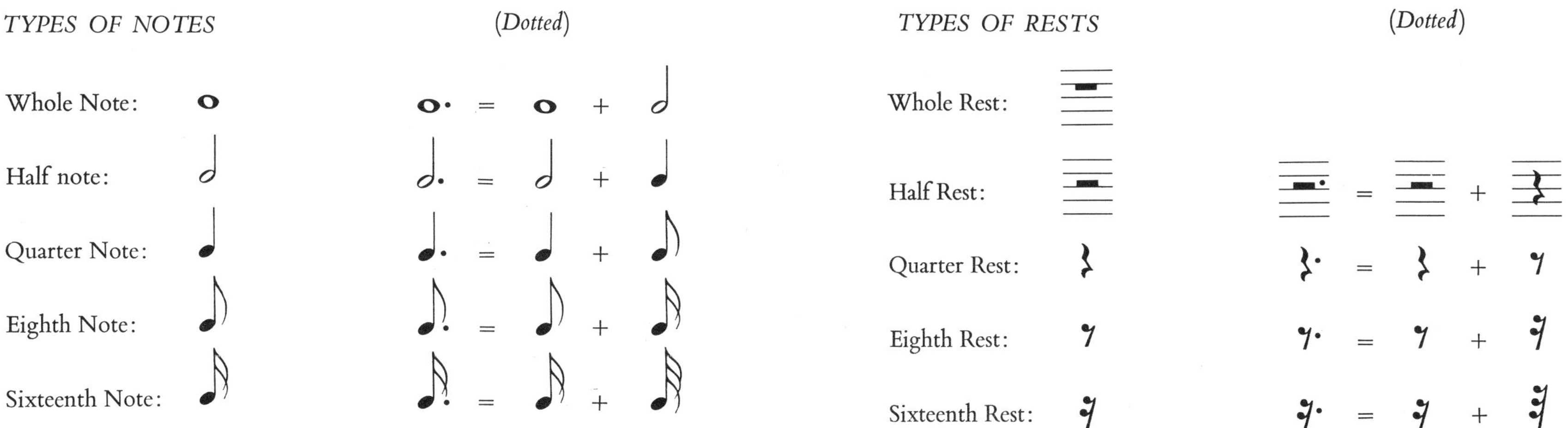

TYPES OF NOTES
(Dotted)
TYPES OF RESTS
(Dotted)
Whole Note:
Half note:
Quarter Note:
Eighth Note:
Sixteenth Note:
Whole Rest:
Half Rest:
Quarter Rest:
Eighth Rest:
Sixteenth Rest:

The following chart shows the subdivisions of a *whole note* down to sixteenth notes:

One *whole note*
is equal to 2 *half notes*
or 4 *quarter notes*
or 8 *eighth notes*
or 16 *sixteenth notes*

2 *Measure and Meter Signature*

Measures are divisions of music into a regular number of beats. On a score they are indicated by vertical bars crossing the staff:

The meter signature, which is shown at the beginning of each piece of music, gives the measurement of the music by supplying two facts. The top number of the meter signature tells the *number of beats in each measure.* The bottom number indicates the *rhythmic value of each beat.* Thus, $\frac{4}{4}$ meter indicates that each measure receives four beats and each beat is the equivalent of one quarter note. $\frac{3}{4}$ meter indicates that the measure has three beats in it, and a quarter note is the beat equivalent. $\frac{2}{2}$ meter indicates that each measure receives two beats and each beat is the equivalent of one half note.

3 *Pitch*

The first seven letters of the alphabet serve to name the various levels of sound, A, B, C, D, E, F, G.

4 *Clefs, Ledger Lines, Staff Spellings*

The diagram below illustrates the *treble clef* (𝄞), the *bass clef* (𝄢), *ledger lines*, and the *staff spelling* of the different pitch names. The illustration below shows the relationship of the different pitches to the piano keyboard.

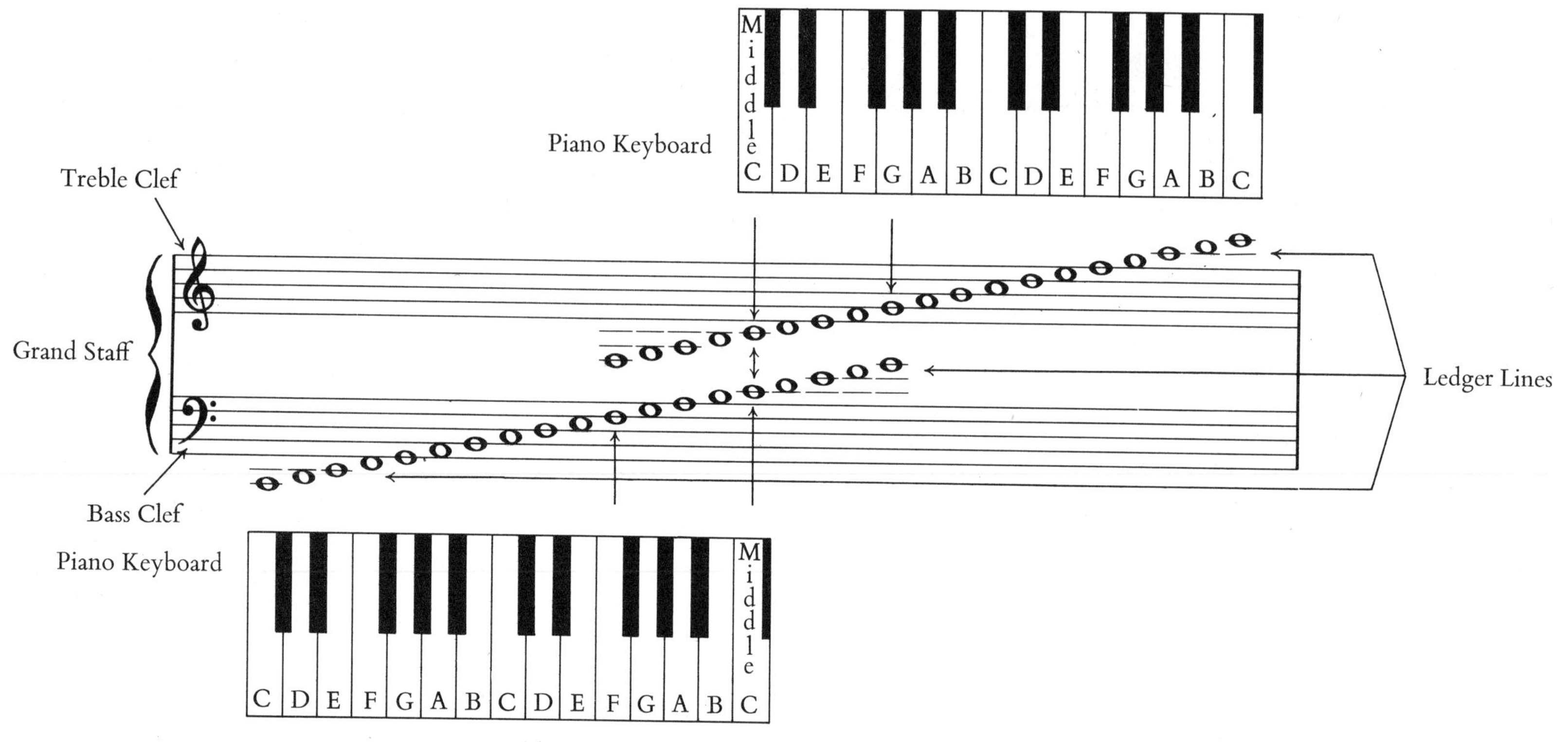

Piano Keyboard
Middle C
C D E F G A B C D E F G A B C
Treble Clef
Grand Staff
Ledger Lines
Bass Clef
Piano Keyboard
C D E F G A B C D E F G A B C
Middle C

5 *Half Steps and Whole Steps*

When two pitches are as close together as possible on the piano keyboard, this constitutes a *half step:*

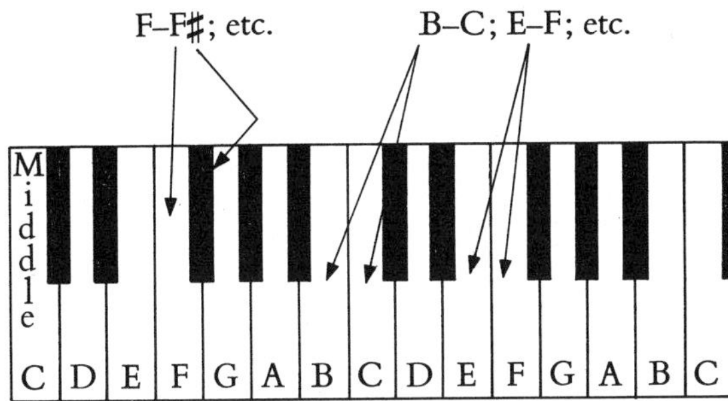
F–F♯; etc.
B–C; E–F; etc.
Middle
C D E F G A B C D E F G A B C

Two half steps form a *whole step.*

6 *Chromatics*

Alterations of pitch are accomplished by making notes sharp, flat, or natural. The written symbols for these *chromatics* are found in the following chart:

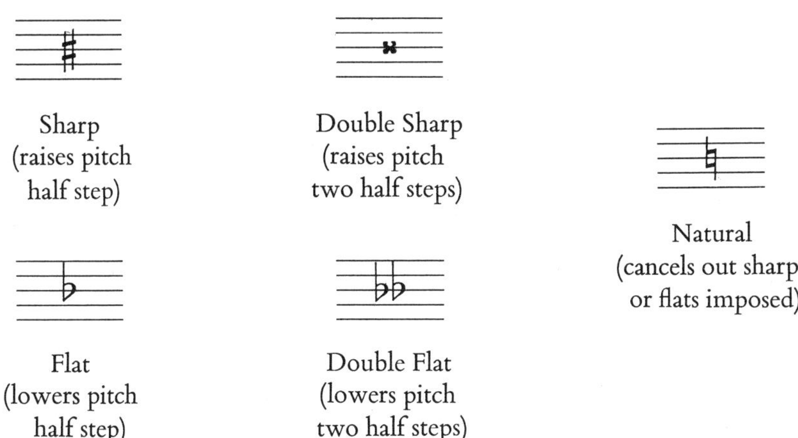
Sharp
(raises pitch
half step)
Double Sharp
(raises pitch
two half steps)
Natural
(cancels out sharps
or flats imposed)
Flat
(lowers pitch
half step)
Double Flat
(lowers pitch
two half steps)

2 Scales

1 *Major*

A major scale is a series of eight pitches in which the whole and half steps between the pitches accords with the following pattern (illustrated by the C major scale):

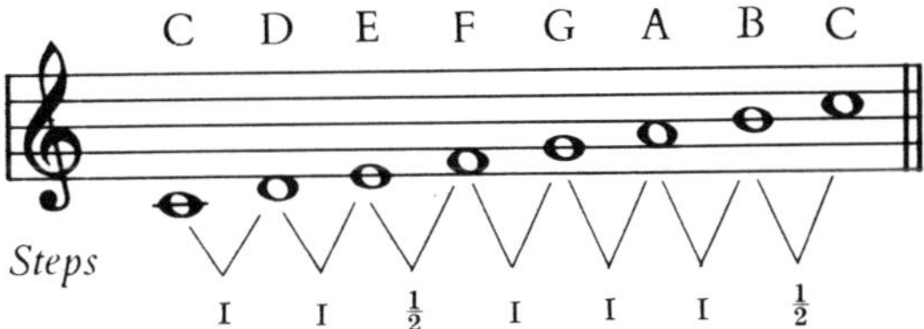
C D E F G A B C
Steps
1 1 $\frac{1}{2}$ 1 1 1 $\frac{1}{2}$

A major scale can be constructed on any tone (white or black key on the piano keyboard) by using the above pattern. The letter names denoting the fifteen major scales (keys) are shown on the *circle of fifths* chart below:

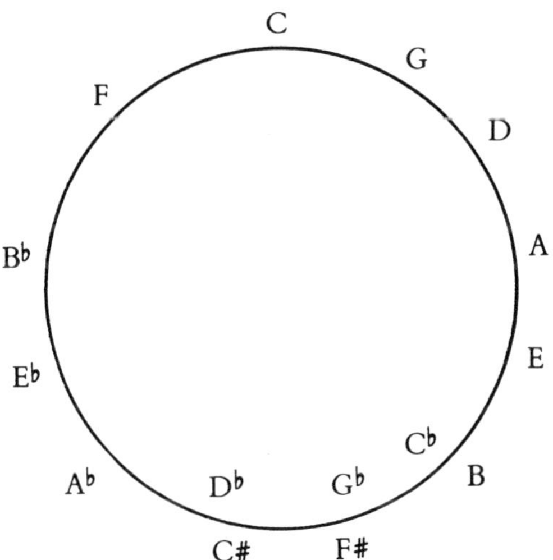
C
G
D
A
E
B
Cb
F#
Gb
C#
Db
Ab
Eb
Bb
F

2 *Relative Minor*

This type of scale is also made up of a series of eight pitches. Each relative minor scale is *related* to a particular major scale. The principal aspect of this relationship is that both the major scale and its relative minor have the same key signature.

There are three different types of relative minor scales: pure, harmonic, and melodic. The key tone (letter name denoting scale or key) is the sixth degree of its relative major scale. For example, the sixth degree of C major is A. Then, A is the key tone of the *relative minor*. The A minor scale is shown below in its three forms, and the relationship of each tone in the series is indicated:

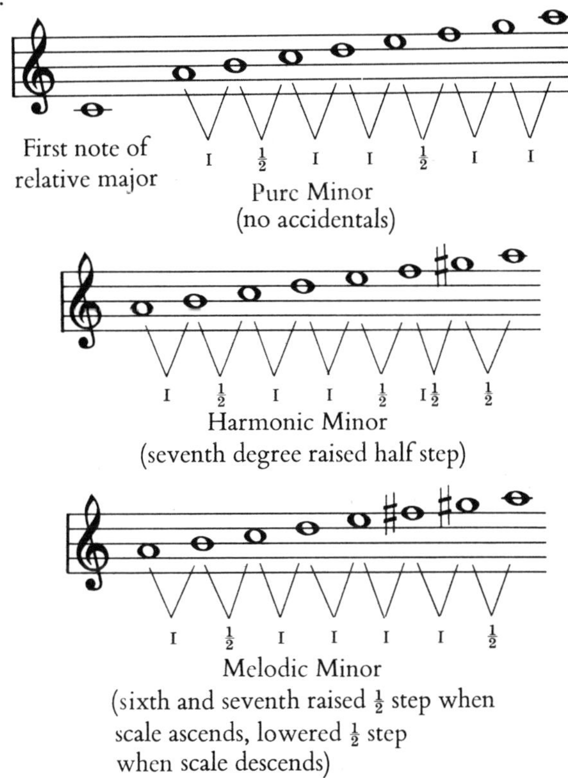
First note of relative major
1 $\frac{1}{2}$ 1 1 $\frac{1}{2}$ 1 1
Pure Minor
(no accidentals)
1 $\frac{1}{2}$ 1 1 $\frac{1}{2}$ 1$\frac{1}{2}$ $\frac{1}{2}$
Harmonic Minor
(seventh degree raised half step)
1 $\frac{1}{2}$ 1 1 1 1 $\frac{1}{2}$
Melodic Minor
(sixth and seventh raised $\frac{1}{2}$ step when scale ascends, lowered $\frac{1}{2}$ step when scale descends)

The *circle of fifths* chart below shows the key tone name of each minor scale relative to each major scale (key). The minor keys are indicated in small letters in parentheses:

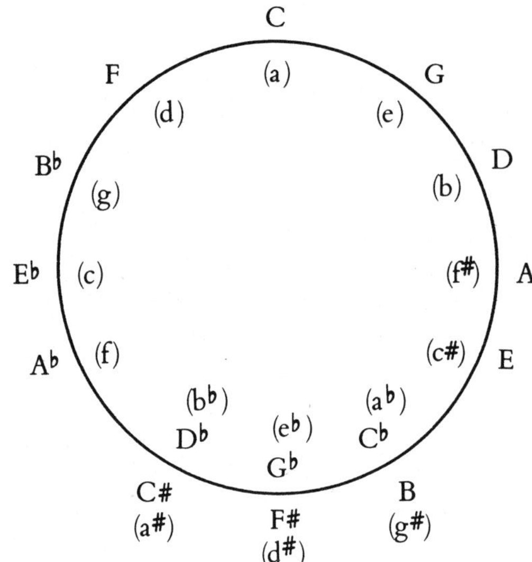
C
(a)
G
(e)
D
(b)
A
(f#)
E
(c#)
B
(g#)
(ab)
Cb
F#
(d#)
(eb)
Gb
C#
(a#)
(bb)
Db
Ab
(f)
Eb
(c)
Bb
(g)
F
(d)

3 Key Signatures

Appropriate chromatics (sharps or flats) are placed immediately following the clef sign on the musical staff to indicate the particular key in which a piece is to be performed. The chart below shows each of the key signatures, with the small letters on top indicating the minor key names, and the capital letters beneath the staff indicating the major key names:

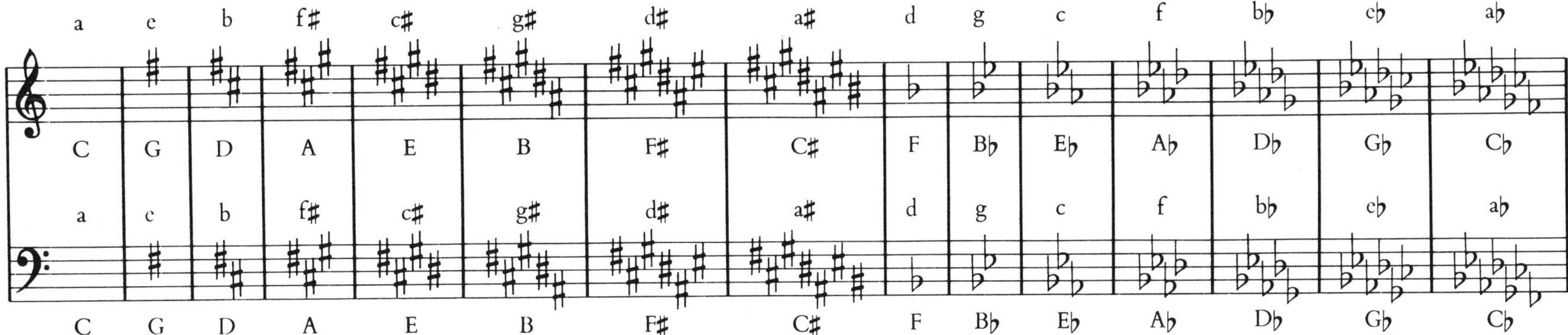
a e b f♯ c♯ g♯ d♯ a♯ d g c f b♭ e♭ a♭
C G D A E B F♯ C♯ F B♭ E♭ A♭ D♭ G♭ C♭
a e b f♯ c♯ g♯ d♯ a♯ d g c f b♭ e♭ a♭
C G D A E B F♯ C♯ F B♭ E♭ A♭ D♭ G♭ C♭

4 Intervals

An interval is the distance between two pitches. Intervals are labeled according to (1) quality and (2) numerical size. Intervals are grouped according to two broad classifications: *major* and *perfect*. All seconds, thirds, sixths, and sevenths are *major* when the top tone is in the key implied by the lowest tone. All unisons, fourths, fifths, and octaves are *perfect* when the top tone is in the key implied by the lowest tone. Intervals derived from the key tone (lowest tone) of C major are shown below:

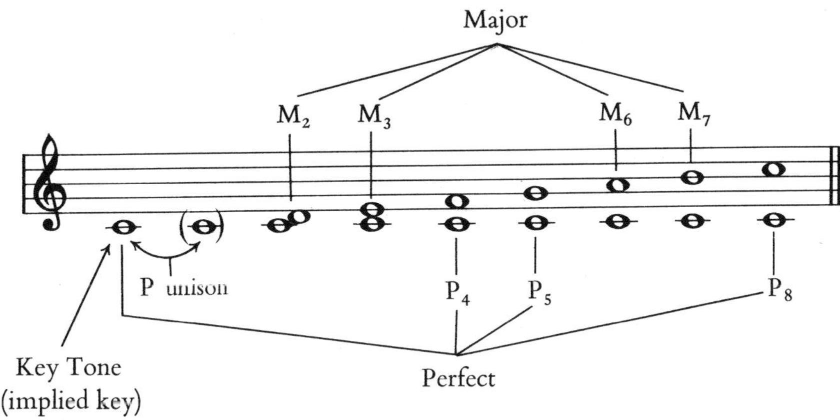
Major
M2
M3
M6
M7
P unison
P4
P5
P8
Key Tone
(implied key)
Perfect

ALTERATIONS

When major intervals have been brought together, or compressed, by one half step, they are called *minor.*

When major intervals have been brought together, or compressed, by a whole step, they are called *diminished.*

When major intervals have been expanded, or opened, by a half step, they are called *augmented.*

When perfect intervals have been brought together, or compressed, by a half step, they are called *diminished.*

When perfect intervals have been expanded, or opened, by a half step, they are called *augmented.*

5 Triads

Each scale degree is referred to by a theoretical name: I (tonic); II (supertonic); III (mediant); IV (subdominant); V (dominant); VI (submediant); VII (leading tone); VIII or I (tonic repeated). Each of these scale degrees serves as a root of a triad (three-tone chord). Triads built on degrees of a major scale are called *major*, *minor*, and *diminished*. Triads built on degrees of the three different relative minor keys are called *minor*, *augmented*, *major*, and *diminished*. The interval composition of each of these kinds of triads is as follows:

Triads	*Intervals*
Major	= M3 + m3
Minor	= m3 + M3
Diminished	= m3 + m3
Augmented	= M3 + M3

Using the C major scale and its relative minor, A, triads have been structured on each scale degree with the quality of each indicated above:

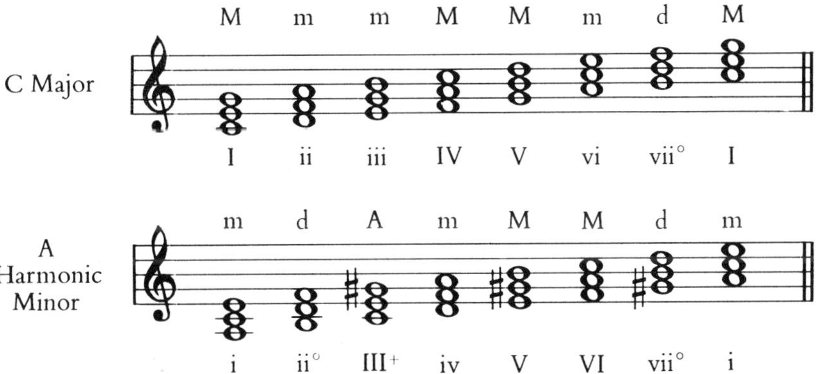
M m m M M m d M
C Major
I ii iii IV V vi vii° I
m d A m M M d m
A Harmonic Minor
i ii° III+ iv V VI vii° i

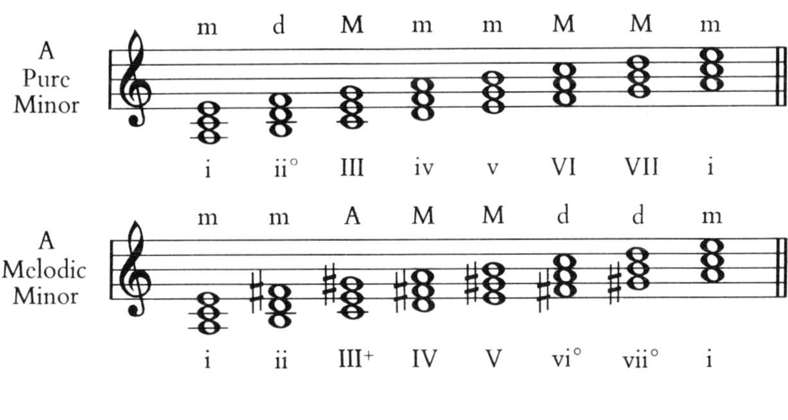
m d M m m M M m
A Pure Minor
i ii° III iv v VI VII i
m m A M M d d m
A Melodic Minor
i ii III+ IV V vi° vii° i

M = major
m = minor
d = diminished
A = augmented

+ = augmented
° = diminished

Appendix B

Tenor Ukulele Tablatures

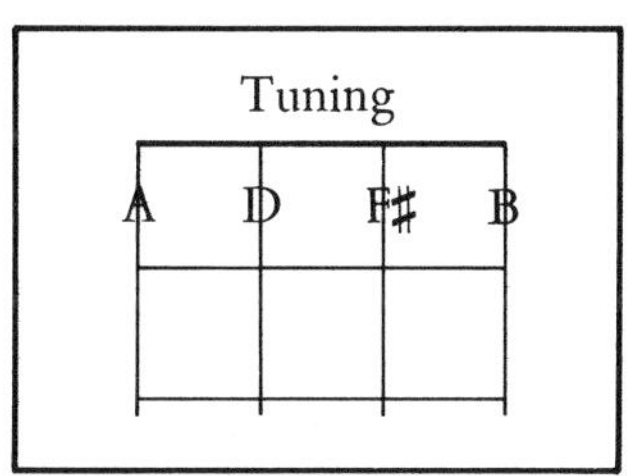
Tuning
A
D
F♯
B

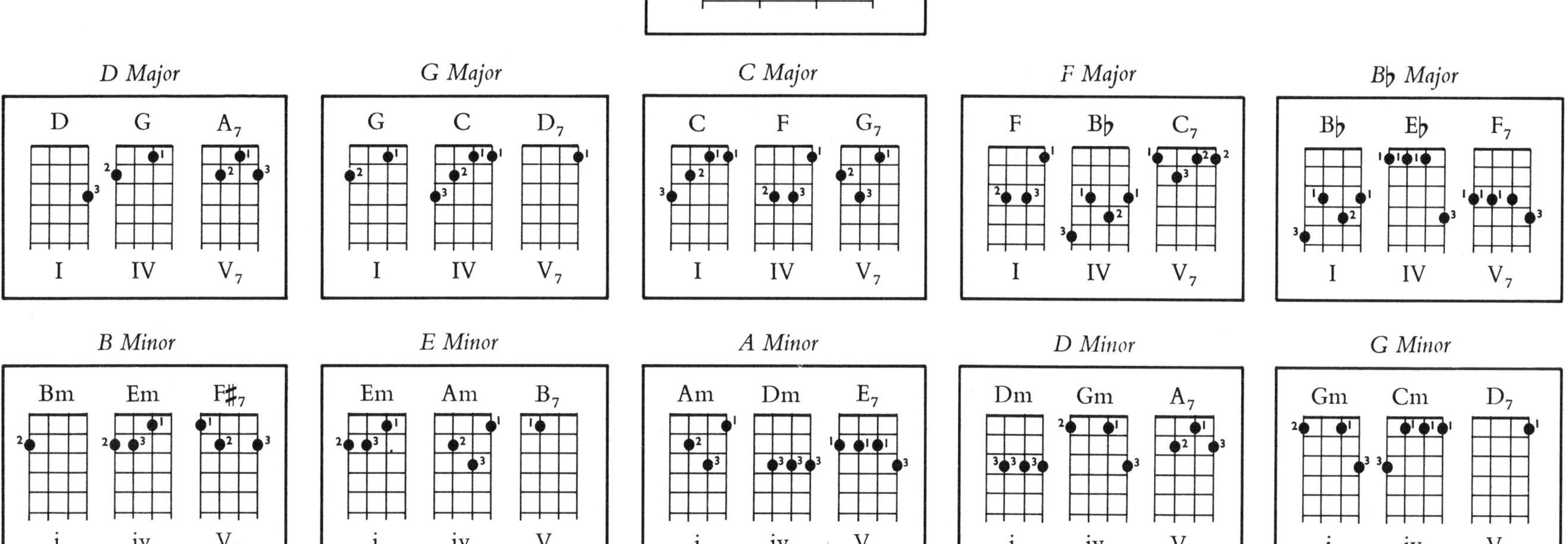
D Major
D
G
A_7
I
IV
V_7
G Major
G
C
D_7
I
IV
V_7
C Major
C
F
G_7
I
IV
V_7
F Major
F
B♭
C_7
I
IV
V_7
B♭ Major
B♭
E♭
F_7
I
IV
V_7
B Minor
Bm
Em
F♯$_7$
i
iv
V_7
E Minor
Em
Am
B_7
i
iv
V_7
A Minor
Am
Dm
E_7
i
iv
V_7
D Minor
Dm
Gm
A_7
i
iv
V_7
G Minor
Gm
Cm
D_7
i
iv
V_7

Index of Songs